MASTERING TRANQUILITY

Books by Nora D'Ecclesis...

Mastering Tranquility

A Guide to Developing Powerful Stress Management Skills

Tranquil Seas

Applying Guided Visualization

Reiki Roundtable

MASTERING TRANQUILITY

A Guide To Developing Powerful Stress Management Skills

by
Nora D'Ecclesis

Copyright © 2011, 2013 by Nora D'Ecclesis

All rights reserved. No part of this book may be reproduced by any mechanical, photographic, or electronic processes, or in the form of an audio recording; nor may it be stored in a retrieval system, transmitted, or otherwise copied for public or private use without written permission of the author. The material in this book is for informational purposes only. As each individual situation is unique, you should use proper discretion, in consultation with a health care practitioner, before undertaking any exercise, recipe, technique or practice described in this book. The author and publisher are not responsible in any manner whatsoever for any injury that may occur through following the instructions in this material. The activities, physical and otherwise, described herein for informational purposes, may be too strenuous for some people and the reader should consult a physician before engaging in them.

Published by Renaissance Presentations, LLC, King of Prussia, PA

Library of Congress Cataloging-in-Publication Data
D'Ecclesis, Nora
MASTERING TRANQUILITY: A Guide to Developing Powerful Stress Management Skills

    1. Stress management 2. Wellness 3. Lifestyle guide

    I. D'Ecclesis, Nora II. Title: Mastering Tranquility

    Library of Congress Registration Number: TX 7-570-038

ISBN-13: 978-0615877044
ISBN-10: 0615877044
Date of First Publication: January, 2012
Second Edition: September, 2013
Printed in the United States of America

Mastering Tranquility is dedicated to the people who taught me compassion, equanimity, love and gratitude

Leanora Pedecine, my Mother
&
Alexander Albano, my Godfather

Table of Contents

Foreword……………………………………………..………....ix

Introduction……………………………………..………..........1

Mind, Body, Spirit, Abundance………………………..….......13

Applying Knowledge To Daily Life…………………………….23

Getting Started: 5 Ways To De-Stress Your Life........................35

The Retreat Experience……………………………...…....47

Meditation: Stopping Mental Chatter ………………....….53

Communication Skills: Passing The Talking Piece…………...73

Yoga: Flexibility Of Body And Mind………………....…....83

Acupuncture: Bringing Energy Flow Into Balance. ..………105

Reiki: Harnessing Energy For Wellness……..…..…..…......117

Exercise: Train Your Body To Function At Its Highest Level.127

Smart Eating: Healthy/Good Recipes From Good People…...149

Homeopathy: Stress Damage Control…………………....…163

Loss & Healing: Handling Life's Most Upsetting Events...….177

Music: The Many Benefits of Playing A Musical Instrument.189

Astrology: Path For The Spirit …………………….............211

Massage: Well Deserved Relaxation……..…..………....…221

Answers To Common Questions……………………….....227

Taking The Next Step…………………………………….....235

Acknowledgements…………………………………….........245

Foreword

My dearest life-long friend has asked me to write a foreword, which I do with delight, because it will give me a chance to embarrass her right at the start. Whenever I introduce Nora D'Ecclesis to someone, I smile and say "oh by the way she is the first woman I was ever naked with." She turns beet red, and then laughing, I quickly explain that we were neighbors, born just a few months apart, and somewhere in an old album is a photo of our mothers smiling, the two of us on our tummies in our birthday suits "sun bathing" between them. If I can ever find that picture I will post it on Facebook for all to see. (My side blotted out of course!)

So with that light opening let's go to serious, for serious indeed is this book. This is a guide book, a primer, a lantern in the dark as to how to take back control of your life and run it in the direction you want it to go. And Nora is the perfect guide.

A bit more about her and I think I can lay claim to if not at least knowing her better than anyone else, I have indeed known her longer than anyone else. From earliest childhood I recall Nora as "the leader." Strong, confident, setting a goal and going straight at it.

As a friend even in earliest childhood she was always there and not just in fair weather. She has been the shoulder I have leaned on more than once in times of great personal tragedy, and her warm embrace has been around me in times of joy. I pray I have been able to do the same for her in all things.

We view how we grew up as a blessing. Our home town was one of the wealthiest suburbs of New York City, but, our little neighborhood of about half a dozen square blocks was literally on the "other side of the tracks," made up of working class folks and recent immigrants. It wasn't the Depression, but it was not a picnic either. Nora endured the terrible tragedy of her father dying young when she was ten, a day I will never forget. And yet that tragedy helped to build the strength she has now. She was blessed with the classic large Italian family of uncles and aunts who stepped in to provide help, love and warmth, and that shaped Nora into a person who understands the true value and gift of helping others, of giving love, of providing warmth.

Time passes, we all grow up, families move, and I so clearly recall the day I was moving away, sitting in Nora's room, the place we so often played together, laughed, cried, argued and made up. We were seventeen and as I got up to leave, we were in tears as we hugged each other goodbye. With nearly all friendships of those years, when you move away, there are promises made that the friendship is forever, but then a week passes, a month, and one day you realize it has become years. That is part of what fuels Facebook, the desire to reconnect with "lost friends" but in most cases, you come to realize that your lives have parted, changed, and that precious closeness has gone.

Not so with Nora. Yes as we went to college, met our spouses, fell in love and married, there were times we would drift apart for a while, but always, like a lodestone, one would draw the other back. And thus it has been for the decades since that day I moved away. Nora went on to her post-graduate studies as did I, we both had single children whom we cherish, she has built a successful business, I went on to become a best-selling author and college professor, but always we stayed close.

And thus to the main reason for this foreword. Why are we close?

As small children Nora could always trump any argument with a fact that could not be disputed. She was four months older than me, therefore knew life better than I did, and therefore was right! And dang it, after all these years she can still use that one, and win, because I realize, she is indeed an "old soul" that actually far transcends a mere four months. She is filled with wisdom and when the deepest of problems hit, ultimately she is the one I will turn to.

Nora has had decades of training in her field and like a high intensity laser-beam she can cut instantly to the core of any issue. And her answer usually is one of tranquility. To seek the stillness that lies within all of us, if only we would let the seas of turmoil calm, and then in that moment of calmness we learn the answers, which in fact are quite simple…But it takes someone with wisdom to see that clearly and help guide you to it.

That is her gift. That is the purpose I see in her life. She is a guide to tranquility and in that tranquility, answers that were there all along, visible just below the surface once the waters have become still and there just below the surface are the truths she can point you towards.

That is the Nora D'Ecclesis I know, from childhood buddy, to guide in life as the journey continues on. As you study with her, and get to know her, you will see that as well, a special something I already knew so many, many years ago.

I thank God she is and always will be part of my life.

William R. Forstchen Ph.D.
Faculty Fellow and Professor of History
Montreat College, NC
New York Times best-selling author.

Introduction

Stress and our reaction to it can kill us.

My dear friend Kathy spoke of this constantly, but neither of us ever really believed those words. It seems her life was filled with far more stress than anyone realized and she did in fact pass in her 40's from what many would consider a stress induced illness.

I also lost my cousin Dr. William Albano to his fourteen hour work-days and the exhaustion of being a surgical oncologist. He passed in his mid-30's from a massive heart attack. My passion was to understand better why this happened to my loved ones and to so many others who lost both quality and quantity in their lives and died so young.

The study of Reiki intrigued me. Energy healing was popular at the time, so my study to become a Reiki Master came first. The Chakras were unknown to me at this point in my life and fascinating to learn. My exposure and study of yoga, meditation, herbal remedies, Chinese Medicine and enhanced communication skills came next.

I learned everything I could get my hands on. Ultimately, I taught others. I soon realized that the best environment to truly absorb these and many other holistic modalities is during a retreat experience dedicated to the total concentration without the external distractions of daily life. They could then be carried back to the real world and incorporated into daily life.

A Bit of Science...

The stress reaction is caused by perceived threats. Like other animals, we have it because it has survival value. When we encounter threatening situations the stress reaction prepares the body for a fight or helps in flight. The reaction starts in the hypothalamus, located in the base of the brain near the pituitary gland. The hypothalamus receives impulses from the cerebral cortex when the senses perceive a threat and sends chemical signals to the adrenal glands which sit on top of the kidneys. The signals tell the adrenals to release epinephrine which increases muscle strength, raises heart rate and increases blood pressure which enables increased power and speed in a fight or flight.

The hypothalamus also tells the adrenal gland to release cortisol, the main stress hormone, which increases blood sugar needed for brain and muscle function in a fight or flight. Cortisol suppresses other non-essential functions not needed in a fight or flight such as digestion and immune function. This alarm system also communicates with parts of the brain that affect fear and mood. Although this is a valuable reaction, if it becomes a chronic state, it may result in significant damage to the body and the mind.

In current times, as opposed to primitive man, such clear cut physical assaults may be unusual but we still feel stress every day simply taking care of our families, commuting in traffic, at work doing our jobs or facing large changes in our lives. Under these circumstances, our stress reaction may be activated almost constantly and cortisol may be elevated for large parts of the day.

Constant stress may result in high blood pressure which has deleterious effects on our heart and blood vessels. It may cause digestive problems, may result in sleep problems, obesity and depression. Deleterious effects on our immune systems may be the worst effects of all. Cortisol suppresses our immune system which leaves us vulnerable to foreign invaders especially viruses. In addition, our immune system constantly seeks out and destroys genetically abnormal cells in our bodies which are forming continually and may eventually develop into cancers.

Impairment of immune surveillance by chronic excess of cortisol may predispose us over time to the development of malignancies. Our immune systems usually identify cancer cells as abnormal by detecting abnormal proteins on their surfaces. These abnormal proteins are present because of the abnormal DNA in the damaged cells. The cells with abnormal DNA are then killed primarily by two types of immune cells called Natural Killer cells and Cytotoxic T cells. Cortisol depletes our bodies of these two types of protective cells.

Viruses may also cause cells to become malignant. Two examples will illustrate this. As we know now, cervical cancer and 25% of throat cancers are venereal diseases. They are caused by HPV (Human Papilloma Viruses), which are transmitted during sexual encounters. The viruses enter cervical cells or cells in the throat during sex and multiplies. Ordinarily, Natural Killer cells and Cytotoxic T cells recognize human cells which have been infected by viruses and kill those particular cells. If, after a number of years, the infected cell is not destroyed, the virus enters the DNA of the infected cell and eventually transforms it into a cancer cell. In most people, these cancer cells are destroyed by NK cells and cytotoxic T cells. As people age, the immune system becomes less effective at identifying cancer cells or virally infected cells, which makes it possible for them escape detection. This is why cancer is more prevalent in older individuals.

Another common virus, the Epstein-Barr virus that causes Mononucleosis, infects lymphocytes and will make the infected lymphocytes immortal. Normally, lymphocytes die after a period of months or years. Again, Natural Killer lymphocytes and

Cytotoxic lymphocytes usually kill these virally infected lymphocytes. If the immune system is impaired by cortisol or by steroid hormones given as medication, the virally infected lymphocytes will proliferate and result is various types of lymphomas or malignancy of lymph nodes.

For optimal quantity of life we should find ways to control stress in our lives if only to decrease undesirable health effects of excess cortisol. Additionally, as we all have experienced at one time or another, chronic stress decreases the QUALITY of our lives. We should learn to eliminate at least some of our daily stress in order that we may approach our lives with equanimity and calm perspective.

The purpose of Mastering Tranquility is to give you some techniques to increase the QUANTITY of your life but perhaps as importantly, its QUALITY.

A Bit of Reminiscence…

My first retreat was in the fall of my junior year of high school.

Our parents gave permission for us to leave the stressors of algebra, chemistry and gymnastics behind and walk across the street to a faith-based retreat program at the local church. Dozens walked out of that high school into the crisp fall weather, running at top speed through the red and yellow leaves, screaming "RETREAT!"

In retrospect, we were skipping class, looking to socialize and mitigate some of the stressors of a highly competitive high school. Stress was not a word we used much back in those days. In fact, as I recall the word for my generation was pressure. We felt pressure to excel and enter the top Eastern universities. The pressure existed to such a degree that everything else became secondary. Naturally, when it came time for retreat, we ran with our fingers pointed toward the sky and sang a retreat song as a means of escape.

We soon learned that these retreats were highly structured. Oddly enough though, even with the intense discipline there was a tranquility that emerged. We learned about religion of course, but also about morals, ethics and the value of community. The spiritual component was wonderful, but without the overused new-age term of "spirituality". On our retreat, the boys grabbed a quick cigarette in the cemetery. The girls prayed and visited the gravestones, where as it turned out, was the resting place of all of my grandparents. It was peaceful, respectful and anything but what could have been considered "stress".

My hometown came complete with the proverbial railroad tract separating the wealthy from the less affluent areas. All students eventually merged into the one small town high school. Growing up with the sons and daughters of CEO's of companies like AT&T, National Geographic, Progresso and Eli Lilly created an extremely competitive academic environment. The children of those parents, as I came to understand, had even more pressure than those of us who were the first generation of college bound children in our families. Ninety-nine percent went on to four-year colleges…mostly Ivy League. Therefore, we all had plenty of stress, which started early for us, but starts even younger for many children these days.

The Christian retreat can be defined in the simplest of terms as a time spent away from one's normal life for the purpose of reconnecting with God. Although the practice of leaving one's everyday life to connect on a deeper level with God – be that in the desert or in a convent – is as old as Christianity itself. The practice of spending a specific time away with God is a more modern phenomenon, dating from the 1520's and St. Ignatius of Loyola's composition of the Spiritual Exercises.

Webster's defines a retreat as a period of group withdrawal for prayer, meditation, study, or instruction under a director – an act or process of withdrawing, especially from what is difficult, dangerous or disagreeable. EXACTLY. As a young student, my first retreat under proper guidance was a withdrawal from a difficult, stressful life and a move toward prayer, meditation and study.

Once in college, I realized that the highly competitive high school that had caused so much pressure to perform, had also prepared me well academically. I obtained my bachelor's degree in three years and went immediately into graduate school. The concept of meditation was a new one in those days, and like most people especially college students, I had no clue how to quiet my mind. During my academic study in graduate school, I was exposed to meditation for the first time.

Transcendental meditation was just beginning to be explored in the United States and I jumped at the opportunity to attend a week-long retreat. It was an amazing learning experience because now I had meditation to use as a new tool. I learned the concept of mantras, read extensively on the subject, and practiced the techniques that later proved so valuable for my future work. That retreat was a period of tranquility that taught me how to manage stressors in the real world.

Several years later, after marriage, having a child and completing my post-graduate education, I finally found time to attend another retreat. By then, I had a better understanding of my attraction to this method of relaxation. This trip was to a retreat facility that combined several styles of mind/body exercise with energy healing techniques. They gave us a variety of options, including attending yoga classes, dancing, whirling, and Reiki. It was my first exposure to Reiki. In addition to being a participant, I also became an observer because the seeds of facilitating my own retreats emerged.

The program I entered that week was called Honoring Women, which included daily lessons with a large group of women from all over the United States. During the class on Honoring Women we introduced ourselves and everyone turned out to be either a yoga instructor or a daily yoga practitioner. I, on the contrary, was a banker. I took some teasing about that, with many asking how I fit in. Obviously, I found that to be a bit strange.

On Saturday morning, we were informed that no caffeine was available because the leaders of the organization decided that it was not a substance they wanted on the premises. Yes, coffee was considered contraband. The friend I attended with desperately wanted a cup of coffee. Being the proactive person that I am, I set out to find some. The first man I asked was the sous chef. The sous chef told me to go down the elevator and walk to the left down a hallway, then turn right, walk to the door at the end of the hallway and knock four times. Then I was to hand the guy who answered the door a twenty-dollar bill and in return, he would give me a pack of Folgers instant coffee.

I thought this was hilarious at the time and still do, but it taught me that individual differences need to be respected at retreats, as they should be in all other areas of life.

My personal special moment that weekend was when I entered the dining hall and asked the man to my left if I could read his newspaper only to be "shushed" by a few dozen people. It seemed that the program leaders decided that the meals would be eaten in silence that day. I was told I could go to another dining room, which turned out to be a small glass-enclosed space that held about a dozen people. I ate there and read and discussed the news of the day. I know that sometimes it is a good idea to omit newspapers during a retreat, but I felt it should be my choice, not the mandate of the administrators.

The next morning, I went directly to that small dining room again, only to get tossed out because on that day it had become the new silent area. This was a very funny moment and a great learning experience for my future leadership at Tranquil Seas Retreats, teaching me that a retreat should be more about the individual participant than the organizer enforcing a rigidly strict program.

On the final day there, the group leader held a pendulum to the heart chakra of every retreatant. She teased me about being a banker, and questioned whether bankers even had hearts. However, my heart chakra was open and clear.

I committed to the study of Reiki at that moment, realizing that holistic studies should be inclusive of people from all walks of life, not just those who conform to a pre-designed paradigm.

At Tranquil Seas Retreats, we use retreat centers and hotels in peaceful areas like the mountains and near the sea. Our participants come from all walks of life. They are informed of any "silent areas" on the premises far in advance. The meals include meat, as well as vegetarian and vegan options. The chefs are chosen because they are excellent and they assist us in planning each balanced meal down to homemade desserts. Coffee which is never viewed as contraband, tea, fruit juice and water are available at all hours. Beginner classes are offered in each subject so that no one feels left out during a particular class. The staff of professionals who make up the administration are highly credentialed in their areas of expertise, and will assist anyone at any level to learn and appreciate the methods to efficient stress relief. They are inclusive of everyone who wishes to learn, and hold no pre-conceived notions of bankers or anyone else.

Mind, Body, Spirit, Abundance

The Four Element Approach:

Mind

Identify and deconstruct your fears.

Body

Strengthen your body, inside and out.

Spirit

Channel the potency of your emotions.

Abundance

Being a part of the universe attaches us to its abundance.

The Importance of Balance

Identifying and deconstructing our fears is vital to enjoying happier, more satisfying lives. To do this requires a systematic approach to examining questions that have been asked by philosophers since ancient times.

Some of the questions we ask ourselves in this pursuit might include: Why am I here on earth? How can I live a happier, calmer life? What is the meaning of my existence? How can I deal with others in a more ethical way?

Consideration of these concepts has a calming effect because it provides a plan or framework for approaching spiritual aspects of our lives apart from solely material goals. Working toward answers to these questions does not require a thorough knowledge of the history of philosophy or the various thought systems of famous philosophers. It only requires that one thinks about them in a serious, mature way. Dealing with these questions makes us all philosophers.

Since the beginning of early civilization, before the written word, people have asked questions regarding the purpose of our existence and the nature of our world. Determining to what extent life has meaning is the primary task of philosophy. The questions were asked because people felt then, as we do now, that there must be more to life than simply going through our daily routine. They want to find a purpose for the efforts they make beyond the pursuit of material things. In addition, they would like to improve the quality of their lives. Without some personal and societal structure, to put it in the words of 17th century British philosopher Thomas Hobbes, we are in a constant state of struggle and life is, "…solitary, poor, nasty, brutish and short." Many philosophers in different times and cultures have arrived at a similar approach to living a calmer and more fulfilling life.

Aristotle, one of the earliest and most significant of any of the philosophers, proposed that a virtuous person lives by the principal of moderation. He said that to be a virtuous person one must perform virtuous acts consistently, not just sporadically. Right, or virtuous, acts are found in the middle of opposite extremes, therefore he urged moderation in all things. The extremes are always evil, whether it is an extreme of deficiency or extreme of excess. For example, if the virtue is courage, the extreme on one side is cowardice and the extreme on the other is recklessness. If the virtue is generosity, the extremes are stinginess on one side and wastefulness on the other. If the virtue is gentleness the vices are indifference on one side and irascibility on the other. If the virtue is friendliness the vices are churlishness on one side and obsequiousness on the other. If the virtue is modesty, the vices are false modesty on one side and boastfulness on the other.

The Epicureans, a sect in Greece that existed shortly after Aristotle's time, held the primary tenet that pleasure is the greatest good in life, a sentiment that has been completely misinterpreted in recent times, causing them to be considered simply pleasure seekers. For the Epicureans, the highest pleasure is simply the absence of pain. You can seek the absence of pain through MODERATION in your lifestyle and by limiting your desires in all aspects of your life including eating, sleeping, working and sexuality. It is easy to see that too much or too little of any of the foregoing will result in pain or discomfort and decrease the quality of one's life.

The principle of moderation has guided ethical behavior for several hundred years in very different cultures. Part of the principle of moderation involves controlling your desires so that they do not rule over reason. External desires are a source of unhappiness but they cannot control you unless you let them. The Stoic philosophers said that you should want what you have. You will be happier wanting what you have than if you continually desire things you do not have.

In the words of Socrates, "The unexamined life is not worth living." Even if one thinks this is overstating the case, it has to be conceded that dealing with philosophical questions adds to the QUALITY of our lives. Although none of us knows in advance the extent of the QUANTITY of our lives, we do have a fairly high degree of control over its QUALITY based on our own day-to-day decisions and by exerting control over our desires. The primary objective of each of us should be to increase the quality of our lives to the greatest extent that we can. In this way we can honor our own existence and add to quality of the lives of those close to us and about whom we care most.

The Aristotelian advice about moderation suggests personal responsibility and rational choices to create the space for balance. This in turn sets into motion the potential for progress toward the serenity of mind, body, spirit and abundance. Balance of these four is the goal.

Equanimity

The word equanimity comes from the Latin word aeguus which means balanced and animus which means spirit.

The ancient Greeks taught:
Nepsis – sober observation
Ataraxia – freedom from upset
Apathia – dispassion

That is the exact goal: a balanced spirit.

With equanimity we learn to fight off reactions to the limbic system's production of cortisol.

Training for equanimity creates tranquility.

If a person wakes to find they have won millions in the lottery and they remain calm and balanced, they have achieved a state of equanimity. Conversely, if that same person has total loss of possessions when their home burns to the ground and remains balanced that is also equanimity. They become observers of the events, free from upset and dispassionate.

Here is an example of equanimity in a typical relationship issue dispute. The wife shops for the perfect ingredients and makes her husband's favorite meal, then cooks the meal which includes preparing the taco meat with fresh spices selected at the gourmet grocery store. The meal is prepared and served with love and attention to detail. Now, on this particular night the wife will not be home for dinner so as she exits passing the husband in the hall she tells him where to find everything and goes on her way. Later that evening, she returns home to find all of the food has been left unrefrigerated, creating the need to dispose of it.

There are many reactions to this situation. One might be what the psychologists call 'unconscious incompetence' where the individual does not understand or know how to do something and does not necessarily recognize the problem. The wife might go upstairs with this reaction and wake up the husband and scream and yell "how could you be so thoughtless and irresponsible?"
Or maybe she got angry but knew to calm down before she talked to him about it. This is called conscious incompetence. Though she does not understand or know how to do something, she does recognize the deficit, as well as the value of a new skill in addressing the problem.

A third type of reaction involves conscious competence where she understands that yelling is not the way to go. However, demonstrating that knowledge requires concentration.

Finally, the best response resulting in equanimity is unconscious competence where the wife demonstrates so much repetition with this that it has become second nature. This results in no reaction at all which is the goal and equals equanimity.

She cleans up the food and goes to bed. Guess which one creates tranquility for the wife? The degree to which equanimity is maintained is the degree to which one is mature. Complete attention to one's own needs is a retreat from maturity.

Love is the ability to put someone else's interest before our own. Living our lives in such a way as to exclude meaningful, mature relationships is to squander the opportunity to participate in the most important experience a human can have.

Relationships require serious and sustained effort that many are unwilling to make. Putting someone ahead of your own interest is difficult to do for a prolonged period but this is exactly what is required in order to preserve and develop a meaningful relationship. Good parenting shows a child how to put another's interest before his or her own. In other words, it teaches the child how to love.

Mature relationships depend on love. Love is a gift. It is given freely by someone. If someone offers us this gift, we may choose to accept it or refuse it. We may desecrate it or we may ignore it. If we do the latter it may be expected that the giver is maybe deeply hurt by our refusal. If we accept the gift and nurture it, especially if the giver is a spouse, it will provide the most rewarding of human experiences.

What is Enough?

Abundance is the direct opposite of scarcity…to have enough. Do we ever feel that we have enough? How do we attract abundance? Sir John Templeton was one of the greatest investment gurus who ever lived. When asked the source of his abundance by Louis Rukeyser on the television program Wall Street Week, Templeton responded: "To tithe".

Sir John begin all of his seminars with a spiritual message with the concepts of service to others and gratitude. He quoted Ben Franklin – "Doing well by doing good" and lived his life consistent with that philosophy. John Templeton gave his time, energy and money while successfully managing his Templeton Mutual Funds for decades. He never had a mortgage or a car loan and was able to do so by saving 50% of his earnings and living on the other 50%. He saved enough as a young man to buy his first small home in cash and made a 28% profit selling it five years later. John Templeton was on to something most Americans do not appreciate today: service first, long term investments and buying only what you can actually afford. His is the formula for attracting financial abundance.

Resource: Templeton, Lauren. Investing the Templeton Way. New York: McGraw Hill, 2008.

Abundance Checks

Set your intention for abundance: Pull a check out of your checkbook or draw one on a piece of paper (at Tranquil Seas Retreats, we provide printed checks).

Within 24 hours of a new moon:

- Write your name in the pay to area.
- Write "Paid in Full" in the dollar amount areas.
- In the signature area, write "The Law of Abundance."

This is a fun tool to attract prosperity which might come in the form of financial abundance, good health, harmonious relationships, or simply a more tranquil life. The ritual has been handed down for so long that its origin is unknown. I use 108 as my check number, because 1 is unity, 0 is wholeness, and 8 is infinity. Good luck!

Applying Knowledge To Daily Life

"Mastering Tranquility" is your guide to the uplifting practices that have helped countless people overcome the debilitating effects of stress. It is a companion for anyone who wants to adapt to the many anxieties, fears, and worries encountered in everyday life by pursuing spiritual fulfillment through revitalizing activities.

From attitude adjustments to yoga practices, whether you choose to specialize in one discipline or take steps into each, the tools and philosophies behind them are provided in simple terms that will allow you to make adjustments to any areas of your life where they are necessary.

As part of the "Retreat Experience" section, brief sample practices are included so that you have structured examples of how to apply knowledge gained to your daily life. The techniques elucidated are designed to be performed in short periods of time so that they will find a place in even the busiest of days. As you have likely realized, it is those extremely busy days that make relaxation techniques much more necessary.

Additionally, both instructors and attendees of Tranquil Seas Retreats contribute observations and anecdotes in our "Illustrative Journals". The Illustrative Journals will help you bridge the gap between theory and application, offering real-life examples from people who have traveled the same path that awaits you.

Where a weekend retreat is concerned, that is a fundamental difference between taking a class, reading a book, or viewing an instructional DVD. While it may be possible to learn a great deal about a given topic in a traditional setting, going on a retreat helps each individual cultivate proper balance by understanding how to interconnect techniques and practices into each day. This amalgamation creates a union of stress-management techniques that are, as a whole, more effective than the sum of their parts.

✎Illustrative Journal: by J.G.M.

Tranquil Seas Retreats have enhanced my life in a myriad of ways that I'd like to consolidate into the 3 Ps: People, Power and Peace. People – each person brings a personality and a passion and amazingly everyone provides help to each other in ways that can never be foreseen. The camaraderie built during the various activities translates to enlightenment. We are all a source of well-being to one another. As a group, the retreats actually build individual power. As the saying goes, knowledge brings power. These retreats dramatically expanded my knowledge in so many areas that I have become a stronger person, both mentally and physically. Experiencing this power surge makes us more capable in the day-to-day environment, personally and professionally. All of this blends to achieve an ultimate goal of peace. I just love the focus on finding ways to internalize peace so I can take this gift and share with others.

Self-Examination

Introspection is a necessary step. It reveals things that may need to be corrected, eliminated, improved, energized or strengthened.

Be honest with yourself.

Admitting that you're fearful of something is nothing to be ashamed of. Fear is often unfairly viewed as weakness, but by applying an approach of non-judgmental self-awareness, you can identify your fears and anxieties, formulate a plan that addresses specifically how you can deconstruct them and reclaim the energy they steal from you.

Be specific.

Identify exactly what puts you in a bad mood. For example, if money or lack thereof is a problem, break down exactly what is happening with your income and spending. Are you spending on credit, purchasing luxury items you don't need? Are you spending it to impress superficial people that don't deserve your attention?

Set goals.

One's ambitions are very unique to the individual. Therefore, for our purposes we will define attainment of a "goal" by the position of where you currently find yourself in life, relative to where you would like to be. Setting attainable objectives is essential to making steady progress. When goals are set in a systematic fashion, adjusted according to results, and followed reliably, there is a much increased chance of an individual achieving success in his or her chosen endeavor.

Though goal-setting is easier when the objective is tangible, progress can still be observed in ventures where the destination is not as clear-cut. For example, if the macro goal is "stress reduction," that particular classification is much too broad. It must be dissected into more manageable parts. The sources of stress can be analyzed rationally and identified. Once that happens, steps should be taken to eliminate the causes. If it is not possible to eliminate them – and of course, it often isn't – a practice of management takes place. Be assured that however daunting the task may seem, it is possible to overcome even the most distressing situations and occurrences.

Recognize your needs.

You are an individual. As such, you have very specific needs. Pay attention to them. While it may seem obvious that an individual should be acutely aware of his or her own needs, it is easily forgotten amidst the steady torrent of unsolicited bad advice that is received throughout the day from assorted co-workers, fair-weather friends, casual acquaintances, and even family members.

Realize that no one knows what is better for you than you do. Accordingly, you should look deep inside yourself and form an opinion about what is necessary to make your life better. When you have arrived at a sensible conclusion, arrive at a series of realistic ambitions.

Set your intention.

Whether the proposed remedy includes twenty-five minutes of meditation per night, a healthier diet, regular yoga practice, or a combination of each, form a plan and implement it. It may be helpful to write it down so you can refer back to it later. This will help you assess progress.

It is the case with most long-term endeavors that staying on track is often the most difficult aspect. This book can help. Select the chapters that will help you to accomplish your goals, then read and re-read them. Simple solutions to common problems are presented, with attention to both short-term and long-term wellness. If you are not sure about one of the techniques suggested in the book, approach it with a degree of skepticism without outright cynicism. Try the discipline in question for a few weeks and see how it affects you.

While it is worthwhile to master dozens of Yoga postures, maybe you'll experience your best results with just four or five postures, practiced a few times per week.

Find what works.

Your results will be highly individual and may require a certain degree of experimentation before you will arrive at the desired level of success. With persistence, short-term goals will adapt into long-term accomplishments. For example, at the time you first read this, maybe you're only able to meditate for two minutes or so before your mind starts to wander. Maybe when performing a forward bend during yoga practice, you're only able to touch your shins. Or maybe you're attempting to learn how to play the guitar and you only know a G chord. Be patient. At first, set your meditation timer for five minutes. A week later, set it for ten. Eventually, you'll work your way up to twenty-five minutes.

Stick to the plan.

Avoid frustration by taking note of the incremental progress you make. If it takes you three months to achieve a properly executed forward bend, it will give you an even greater sense of accomplishment than if you are able to do it on your first try. If you're a beginning guitar player and only able to progress at the rate of learning one new chord per month, don't worry that you're moving too slow; instead concern yourself with the progress you're making by setting an achievable, realistic goal. After all, at the rate of one new chord per month will give you a collection of twelve chords at your disposal after a period of one year. Those twelve chords will allow you to learn and perform much of the popular music of the past fifty years.

If it takes one year of steady progression to acquire tools that will serve you for a lifetime, that is a winning proposition.

Conversely, it may not take a year, or even a month to see progress. Take an age-old Eastern tradition like Qigong for example. This might be the first time you've even seen the word "Qigong" in print. However, it is not unreasonable to expect results after one very short Qigong set.

Make your ego work for you, not against you. No matter the period of time that it takes you to advance, enjoy the process, and enjoy your progress.

Motivate yourself.

Motivation means different things to different people. It comes from many sources – from within, from the support of others, from ideas and actions. What is always constant however, is that the will of a person to allow his or her self to become motivated when the stimulus necessitates it. Before each activity, sit down quietly and focus on the value you hope to gain.

Overcome obstacles.

Our goal is to put you in control of properly handling the inevitable challenges that life is full of, and doing so with attention not only towards maintaining and surviving stress, but advancing and progressing in the midst of it. If you feel like you are getting sidetracked, review your goals. Be patient, consistent and live for the moment. If you can adhere to these simple guidelines, you will find yourself always moving forward and taking pride in your accomplishments.

You are not alone.

Whether you are attending a Tranquil Seas Retreat, or simply relaxing in the comfort of your quiet meditation space, this book will assist you like a trusted friend – instructing, motivating, and assisting your ever evolving transformation into the physically and emotionally balanced, spiritually advanced being you are destined to become.

✎**Illustrative Journal: by Jeannie F.**
My first experience with Tranquil Seas Retreats came at a time in my life where I was starting to reflect on my own path and not just that of my children, grandchildren and hubby. I loved them all so dearly, but knew it was time for finding me. I was a little unsure of myself and was questioning what this adventure would be like. I'd met and gotten to know some of the ladies that attend these retreats and so, I took a leap of faith. The leap of faith landed me in the middle of a group of awesome ladies, beautiful serene surroundings and breathtaking views. The beautiful Pocono Mountains set up a solace that my soul needed to open up

and learn. At my first retreat, we had palm readings, Reflexology, Reiki, Yoga, meditation, and other programs throughout the weekend. We attended a wonderful event at Columcille Megalith Park, hiked the woods and started out each day with Tai Chi. My leap of faith brought me to a wonderful place, with wonderful people. I've attended many retreats, since my first and have loved every time I've gone.

Many of us desire for change in our lives, but are unsure how to proceed.

Begin by affirming concepts that are essential, yet often forgotten or ignored.

Relax and refocus.

Appreciate what you have instead of dwelling on what you don't.

Remember that change is inevitable.

Break with old patterns that hold you back from your potential.

Prevent negative thoughts and negative people from controlling your life.

Embrace optimism.

The Need For Adaptation

In 1936, scientist Hans Selye published a paper titled "A Syndrome Produced by Diverse Nocuous Agents". His premise was that the human body goes through a set of responses and adaptations after exposure to stress. The human body is exposed to a variety of stressors, such as pain, extreme temperatures, infections, and of course, emotional strain. Even though the causes of stress can vary widely, its manifestation is the same. The three stages of Selye's General Adaptation Syndrome are:

(1) Alarm
(2) Resistance
(3) Exhaustion

The three stages of General Adaptation Syndrome can be illustrated by the example of sun exposure.

Stage 1 – Alarm: Skin heats up, and the body prepares melanin.

Stage 2 – Resistance: With continued exposure, the body adapts by creating a suntan.

Stage 3 – Exhaustion: When exposure becomes more than the skin can handle, severe redness and burns can occur.

Up to a point, we are able to resist the external strains that are encountered. For example, even in extreme temperatures, the body resists changing its internal temperature unless the conditions persist for a sustained period of time. Even though freezing temperatures are potentially deadly, we have effective methods for dealing with the circumstances. Solutions are obvious: Wear warm clothing. Build a fire. Go inside the house and turn up the thermostat. But what if the set of stressors you encounter isn't so simple? What if the solutions aren't so obvious? What happens when we change the words "extreme temperatures" to "unpaid bills," "failing relationship," or "seriously ill spouse"? More serious circumstances will require a greater effort to combat the challenges that anxiety and tension will put your mind and body through. While preventive maintenance is a must, learning to adapt when times are at their worst is a practice that can be life-saving.

Fortunately, stress management is a skill that can be mastered.

How? Read on.

Getting Started

Building a balanced life begins with eliminating stressful actions and cultivating good ones. There is no reason to wait. Choose to begin the lifelong process of cultivating and cherishing your well-being, and choose to make the commitment immediately.

The intention of these pages is to provide an easy to follow template with the objective of working towards physical, emotional, and spiritual wellness. While the following chapters are full of techniques that you can use to improve the quality of your life over the long term, what you will find below are five suggestions that will, if put into practice right now, produce an immediate difference in your day-to-day life. The common thread between them is simplicity. The shelves of bookstores are filled from wall-to-wall with overcomplicated solutions to the issues we will confront in the following pages. It is over-complication that prevents progress. In the 14th Century, English theologian William of Occam reasoned that "It is vain to do with more what can be done by fewer." Several centuries later, those words are still extremely significant.

If so desired, this very moment can be the beginning of a new era in your life. Ignore poor choices you have made in the past – yesterday exists only in your mind – and embrace the here and now. The only reality is the one we exist in right at this very moment. Live in the moment, and make informed choices that will make every subsequent moment a step in the direction of your personal goals. This type of attitude will make both the journey and the destination more rewarding.

You owe it to yourself to take proper care of your mind, body and spirit. In just a short period of time each day, it is possible to dramatically alter the course of your life in an exceptionally positive direction.

Let's take the initial steps forward.

5 Ways To De-Stress Your Life…Starting Right Now

(1) Devote yourself to improving your health

Investing in your body's long-term wellness begins with the consumption of a sensible, balanced diet. Your nutritional intake affects every part of your life, from your energy level, to your body composition, to your sleeping patterns. Educate yourself on the subject of nutrition, accumulating knowledge from many sources, not just a single book about a particular fad diet. Account for your individual needs and goals, and come up with a nutrition plan that suits you. Stay with the plan, and remember that the two minutes of enjoyment you derive from eating a pastry isn't worth the complications that can follow.

Exercising the body is essential.

The benefits of regular exercise are too numerous to list here, but it is sufficient to say that after just a few weeks on a fitness program, your mind and body will thank you. Engage in physical activity at least three times per week, even if it's as simple as walking your dog for 30 minutes after dinner. There is absolutely no excuse for ignoring physical fitness. For those that don't have time, then make time. At minimum, eliminate 90 minutes a week of unproductive activities and replace them with 3, 30-minute exercise sessions. It's as simple as getting on a stationary bike while you watch the nightly news, or taking the time you would normally spend talking on the phone and meeting your friend in the park for a walk.

Exercising the mind is also essential.

As we nourish and stimulate the body, we must also nourish and stimulate the mind. This is easy to accomplish through activities such as meditation, reading, or a variety of creative pursuits, including drawing, crafting or music.

Any intellectually challenging conversation will also do the trick. Intellectual stimulation through social interaction will not only preserve and expand your cerebral side, but it will increase the respect your peers have for you; a pleasant side-effect of the never-ending journey of personal development.

Becoming conversant in a variety of topics will allow you to engage in more meaningful dialogues with members of your community. Something as simple as joining a book club will introduce more positive energy to your life. Taking a weekend class at a community college will reward you well beyond the couple of hundred dollars it costs to enroll. If the vast majority of people devoted half the attention to discussing art or literature as they do gossiping or following the undertakings of insignificant pseudo-celebrities via "reality" television, their lives would be better for it.

(2) Define the most important tasks for each day

Few notions will serve you more faithfully than a clearly defined plan on how to move forward.

We have a limited amount of time to spend in this great world. Don't waste any of it.

Find simple ways to solve problems, so you will have more time to spend with loved ones and doing things you enjoy. Don't allow yourself to get bogged down by inconsequential details – Instead, accomplish what you set out to do first, then decide if it's in your best interests to take on additional responsibilities.

Here is a technique that will prove helpful in removing life's constant distractions – in addition to making your "To Do List," make lists of the things you want to avoid. For Example:

"To Do" List
☑ Return phone calls from customers
☑ Grocery shopping
☑ Pack suitcase for Tranquil Seas Retreat

"Don't Do" List
☒ Don't let people blame me for things that are their own fault
☒ Don't take repeated phone calls from unreasonable people who waste my time and energy
☒ Don't complain about problems without taking the necessary steps to correct them

You'll notice that the "Don't Do List" will often result in a clearer view of what is important in life than a "To Do List". The reasoning is simple. Think of something as simple as your morning drive to work. Even though the task at hand is to get in your car and commute to your office, getting to the office is actually secondary to your safety; i.e. not crashing your car on the way there. While this case in point may seem ridiculously obvious, as scenarios become less black and white and more shades of gray, it becomes increasingly difficult to distinguish exactly what would be analogous to crashing the car and what would be the equivalent to reaching your destination. The solution is a clear definition of your purpose, arrived at through coherent reasoning. Once your purpose is distinct, the steps along the journey will become almost effortless.

(3) Set boundaries

It is not necessary to make yourself available to absolutely everyone at all hours of the day and night. Designate hours for business activities, especially if you're self-employed or work during unconventional hours. Even if you love your career, make sure you take enough time off from work to ensure proper balance.

Turning off your cell phone at designated times can help. Most cell phones have a "custom alerts" setting that allow you to shut off contact from all people except the callers you designate. If you have children, or anyone in your direct care, set your phone profile to only accept calls from the people who are your priorities. This ensures that they will be able to contact you in the event of an emergency.

Aside from the extremely important people in your life, there is no need for your business associates and friends to have access to you twenty-four hours a day. How many times have you been agitated late at night by disruptive phone calls that could have easily waited until the morning to be addressed? Just because work is someone else's top priority, doesn't mean they should be granted the power to decide whether it should be yours.

Choose what times of the day you will set aside for you and your loved ones, and then adhere to the plan. Many cell phones include an option that will automatically switch to a passive ringtone setting at designated hours.

Your time is valuable and belongs to you, so make good use of it.

Examples of instances that you can enhance with a little extra peace and quiet:
- Sunday dinner
- Meditation
- Before bed

(4) Make the most of your opportunities to rest

The body repairs itself during sleep. Sleep deprivation can lead to innumerable health problems and reduce the ability of the mind and body to function at its highest level. Lack of sleep increases Cortisol levels. Cortisol is, of course, a hormone that consumes muscle tissue and increase fat tissue. Insufficient sleep also decreases sensitivity to insulin, which means the ability to turn food carbohydrates into energy will be hampered and those carbohydrates become more likely to be stored as fat.

I will assume that you are likely already motivated to be preparing your most comfortable pillow by now, let's proceed to some tips on how to achieve better sleep.

Tips to achieve better sleep:

■ Make an effort to get to bed at an earlier hour, which maximizes the time you have to achieve the desired eight hours per night of sleep. Short on time? Cut corners somewhere else, because your health isn't worth jeopardizing over any of the tasks that are keeping you up late. Like your Mother told you, "Get to bed early."

■ Follow a routine of getting to bed at the same time each night, particularly if your alarm clock wakes you at the same time every weekday. Keeping on a regular sleep schedule on weekdays will help your body form a habit of restful sleep.

■ Reduce caffeine consumption by late afternoon. In the evening, switch to Chamomile Tea to take advantage of its calming effect. While caffeine has been shown to have several positive effects, such as decreased likelihood of depression, increased athletic performance, and a high concentration of anti-oxidants, facilitating restful sleep is not among its benefits. Cutting off caffeine 5-7 hours before bedtime allows the body to metabolize and eliminate it from the system.

■ Eat a light, low-calorie snack before bed containing a small amount of protein. Try a hard-boiled egg, mixed nuts or yogurt. It will help the body to regenerate itself, and eliminate the unpleasant "empty stomach" feeling that makes restful sleep difficult. Additionally, it will help to keep blood sugar levels regulated overnight, which will result in a more energetic feeling in the morning.

■ Make your bedroom as dark as possible. At night, block out as much external light as you can, or use a sleep mask if street lamps or other outdoor lighting make the task difficult. Not only will a very dark bedroom make sleep easier by assisting your body's natural rhythms, but it will help to avoid health problems that research studies have associated with sleeping primarily in lighted conditions such is the case with people who work night shifts and are forced to sleep during daylight hours.

■ A reasonably cool temperature of about 67 degrees Fahrenheit is optimal for sleep. Just think of all the stiflingly hot summer nights you've been through that made an uninterrupted night's sleep nearly impossible. Accordingly, use a fan or air conditioning in the summer and avoid setting the thermostat too high in the winter. It's much more conducive to better sleep to regulate cooler temperatures with socks and blankets than it is tossing and turning in a bedroom that is uncomfortably hot.

■ Avoid drinking alcoholic beverages within 4 hours before bedtime. Contrary to what many people who partake in "nightcaps" might believe, alcohol disrupts sleeping patterns if someone is full of it at the time they fall asleep. The "cravings" produced by the body when it wears off will make it difficult to produce sustained periods of REM sleep.

■ If you are prone to serious insomnia, begin to write down all variables in a log book – such as time you went to bed, what you ate prior, etc. Doing so will give you a better understanding of your body's needs and what it responds to, and will also help eliminate causes of poor sleep.

■ The bedroom is for sleep, intimacy with your partner, and getting dressed. Leaving it for those three things will help you focus on the goal. Avoid making the bedroom a television room, workout room, storage space or anything else distracting. Let entry in your bedroom at 11pm be your body's signal that it is time for rest.

(5) Don't Over-Complicate

Simplify.

The Retreat Experience

The experience that participants of Tranquil Seas Retreats encounter is both unique and varied. First time attendees will encounter innovative approaches to stress management, and repeat retreatants will build on the core knowledge attained, as well as gain exposure to new ideas via cycling of the programs ancillary courses. Our events are designed as samplings of relaxing activities that will lead people into longer term interests. However, someone experienced in something such as yoga will find that the nuances elucidated during class will have an expansive effect on their practice. Not only will you develop new interests, but your current interests will blossom as well.

In the following chapters, you will find a selection of the core activities and teachings that one would encounter at a Tranquil Seas Retreat. *We'll begin with a sample weekend program:*

Friday
2:00pm – Check-in
3:00pm – Orientation
4:00pm – Yoga

6:00pm – Dinner

7:00pm – Guitar Workshop

-or- Historical Religions: Taoism in Program Room

8:00pm – Q & A with Seminar Leaders

Saturday

7:30am – Qigong on Mountain Overlook

8:00am – Breakfast

9:00am – Life Transitions

10:00am – Reiki

11:00am – Guided Walk to Mountaintop

12:00pm – Lunch

1:00pm – Walking Meditation

2:00pm – Megalith Park

4:00pm – Yoga

6:00pm – Dinner

7:00pm – Guided Meditation

8:00pm – Breakout Sessions: Yoga Philosophy, Chakra Clearing, Chair Massage Techniques

Sunday

7:30am – Qigong on Mountain Overlook

8:00am – Breakfast

9:00am – Guided Meditation

10:00am – Yoga

11:00am – Closing Ceremony

As is evident from the sample itinerary, the style at Tranquil Seas Retreats is to take a diverse approach, designed to allow people to discover new methods to realize their potential. The activities are scheduled to be near non-stop throughout the weekend, but it is your time to do what you please with, and if you wish to spend an hour or two sitting on the back deck gazing down the mountainside, then that is very much encouraged. In fact, it stands to reason that once we get away from the grind of our careers and into the quiet of the natural landscape, we are able to gain a tremendous amount just from quiet reflection.

Whether learning in class, pensively reflecting in solitude, or socializing with your peers and developing new friendships, a well-organized retreat will provide you with every opportunity to enrich your life.

✎ **Illustrative Journal: by Helen Davis**

The program design was outstanding! Yoga prepared our minds and spirits to make the transition from the outside world to "being" in the place of the retreat. Topics of comparative practices were informative, just the right length of presentation time, and provided us with something new, of value, and that could be applicable to our daily lives.

Given the amount of loss the world has experienced over the past year, the choice of bringing Toni, a grief counselor, as a keynote speaker worked. She gave me an opportunity to examine loss from a broader perspective, have compassion and empathy for others having this experience and to leave with an uplifted spirit.

We were given a choice of breakout sessions – all interesting! The size of the group was small enough to be able to get to know each other and large enough to experience representation from different walks of life.

Begin With Positive Intention

Intention is a resolution to act in a certain way with clarity and with an end goal in mind.

When I decided to go to college I prepared by taking college prep classes. I applied for admission to several universities and tested for scholarships. After I matriculated the path seemed easy to accelerate and graduate with a Bachelor's Degree in three years so that I could seek employment and continue with graduate school.

I had a goal driven by a need and set clear intention. Many people take the exact same path and then after graduation think that intention or goal setting is no longer needed. It is, and many should have an even more intense place in our daily lives.

At the start of my career during a seminar in marketing skills I constructed my first vision board many years ago. I take that board to my retreats as an example of how to construct one, but more importantly to look at the way in which intention is set.

Prior to making vision boards or walking the labyrinth, the retreat group is taught to ask themselves what they want, to establish their goals and set a path to achieve them. Then they imprint them through the labyrinth experience and onto their vision board. The results are phenomenal.

Constructing A Vision Board:

A vision board is a collection of images that have been fastened to a poster-board. The images selected are those which represent what you want from your future. The board is then displayed where it can be viewed on a frequent basis, allowing your goals to come into focus.

Surround yourself with images of your goals, making a visual display of what you want your life to become. Representing your ambitions in a visual way will allow your subconscious mind to focus on positive emotions instead of negative ones.

Go through magazines and select images of what you want to achieve.

Glue the pictures to your vision board.

Add writing if desired.

Hang your vision board in a visible place.

Viewing it will give your desires focus and clarity

Meditation

Stopping Mental Chatter

Silencing the mind by meditative concentration is increased by the silence creating the inner peace that opens the door to one-pointed meditation. While meditating we target something for the mind to concentrate on, which will give tranquility. The targeted effects of reciting a mantra, watching a candle burn, visualizing a cresting wave over and over again, or simply concentrating on breathing creates the environment for serene meditation from consciousness to super consciousness. One should start with ten minutes a day, and progress to twenty.

Meditation is usually performed regularly in the morning and evening. It may be performed alone, or in a group. It involves sitting in silence with the back straight and centered, keeping the body still, taking deep breaths, and keeping the mind still. Seated meditation is a practice of sitting in stillness that ultimately allows us to experience a higher awareness. During the day's activities, try to remind yourself to keep proper posture with the back, similar to the posture taken when meditating. This helps keep focus on the activity at hand, and the effort of engaging in good posture helps quiet the mind during a stressful day.

The calming effects of meditation can impact you positively both mentally and physically by reducing stress, increasing energy and enhancing mental clarity. Meditation focuses the mind's attention on a certain thought or feeling. Accordingly, when meditating, focus on what you want, not on what you don't. Keep an inward mental focus. Focus allows the mind to concentrate without interference from other outside thoughts. Looking inward can help improve your connection with the external world. Visualization focuses the mind's attention on an act or movement, making a connection between the imagination and subconscious.

How to Meditate:

Find a quiet place.

Eliminate distractions such as cell phones, television, and computers.

Get comfortable.

Choose a comfortable position, preferably one of the following:
Upright on a chair
On a cushion
Cross-legged
Lotus or Half-Lotus posture

Burmese seated position
Kneeling, with the posterior on a bench or supported by cushion

Keep a straight back.

Focus your attention on breathing or a Mantra. A mantra can be a poem, prayer, phrase, chant or word.

Center breathing on the Hara line which is the line that runs vertically up the center of the body.

If the mind wanders, bring it back to your breath or mantra.

Focus on positive thoughts and/or visualize a tranquil setting.

It may be helpful to set a timer if so desired when it is time for you to re-enter full consciousness.

Walking Meditation

Labyrinths are ancient human symbols known to go back at least 3,500 years. They appeared on most inhabited continents in prehistory, with examples known from North & South America, Africa, Asia and across Europe from the Mediterranean to Scandinavia. The labyrinth symbol was incorporated into the floors of the great Gothic pilgrimage cathedrals of France in the twelfth & thirteenth centuries. An example of a famous design is the nave floor of the Cathedral of Notre Dame de Chartres outside of Paris. This labyrinth was built of honey-colored limestone with marble lines around the year 1200.

Walking in a labyrinth is walking meditation. The use of intuition when walking the path is a right brain task. If a person elects to enter they are clearly making a choice toward a spiritual path that is represented by the labyrinth structure. It might be said that walking into the labyrinth is a metaphor for walking toward your core. Labyrinths are described as being "unicursal" – when you walk in and around the way out is the exact same way in. It is not a maze or puzzle to be solved; a labyrinth is a path in and out.

Research conducted at the Harvard Medical School's Mind/Body Medical Institute by Dr. Herbert Benson has found that focused walking meditations are highly efficient at reducing anxiety and eliciting what Dr. Benson calls the 'relaxation response'. This effect has significant long-term health benefits, including lower blood pressure and breathing rates, reduced incidents of chronic pain, reduction of insomnia, improved fertility, and many other benefits. Regular meditative practice leads to greater powers of concentration and a sense of control and efficiency in one's life. Labyrinth walking is among the simplest forms of focused walking meditation.

✎Illustrative Journal: by Barbara Snow

I have had the pleasure to attend several Tranquil Seas Retreats in Kirkridge, PA. Most of these retreats have been held at Nelson Lodge, which sits up high on a mountaintop overlooking the valley below. These retreats always offer a little of everything….Reiki, Qigong, Yoga, massage, palmistry, hiking the trails, and walking the labyrinth. There is also a different guest speaker at each retreat. Everyone looks forward to breakfast, lunch and dinner because they are all homemade meals and absolutely outstanding which is one of the reasons we keep returning. The afternoon we arrived at Kirkridge for the December, 2010 retreat we were given beads, some large and some small, to craft Mala beads to take with us when we went to walk the labyrinth. I thought that it was going to be a really easy project but it ended up taking several hours as the ends kept fraying and it was very hard to get the end thru the small beads. All said and done they turned out to be very beautiful. The following day I had my Mala beads along with my magnet and with each step I just kept repeating the saying over and over again while walking the labyrinth. It is hard to explain to someone who has never seen or walked a labyrinth the wonderful energy and the spirituality that one feels while walking it. I look forward to walking the labyrinth each time we go back on retreat.

Guidelines For Walking A Labyrinth:

Pause at the entrance to center yourself

Keep your mind receptive

Walk with purpose and focus

Pause at the center to open your mind to new insights

After exiting the Labyrinth, reflect quietly on your experience

✒Illustrative Journal: by Sheryl M.

A labyrinth is representative of the path that is walked in life. Whenever I enter the Labyrinth at Kirkridge, I pause, clear my mind and set the intention to be open to any insights which may come up. I also include appreciation of a peaceful experience, if it turns out to be a walking meditation without any insights. I try not to desire one over the other.

I have had several meaningful insights while walking the labyrinth there. I realized that walking a labyrinth is like traveling through life. We encounter bumps in the road. We might have no idea whether our path is the right one – we just have to trust that our intuition is correct. We encounter other people on parallel paths. We might not see the other people on parallel paths until we come to a crossroad. We might get lost on our journey, even though the path is well marked and everyone says it's impossible to get lost. The journey might seem long one time and very short the next – even though it is in reality the same distance. We might be so intent on getting to the end that we miss the subtle sounds, sights, smells of Nature.

We can be very oblivious of the people around us, or we can be too distracted by what they are doing and forget where we are going. If we are mindful, we notice the small signs that others have passed this way before us – a footprint, a memento left lovingly behind, a stone dislodged by a wayward boot. I notice my inclination to make everything perfect again…to straighten the stone, to erase the footprint. I notice my desire to make the path safe for the next traveler. To question whether it is safe up ahead for all of us…I always note the rhythm of my feet walking, the crunch of the stones, the peaceful feeling of relaxing into walking meditation, letting my breath and feet do what they naturally will. The swaying of my body as I make a turn, following the carefully placed stones. I appreciate the sense of calm within that stone circle. I acknowledge the sacredness of the space, cleansed by many feet silently stepping, spiraling through the small path. I feel the connection to all who have traveled this path, and especially to those on it with me. And I hope I will always be so mindful on my own Path.

Kirkridge & Columcille

Kirkridge Retreat Center is a very special place to many participants of Tranquil Seas Retreats and the most popular and frequent of our retreat destinations to date. Bob Raines, the former director of Kirkridge, used to say these words on the first night of a retreat:

The mountain welcomes you to Kirk-ridge church on the Appalachian ridge. This ancient rock has been here for 300 million years. Whatever sin or sorrow, grief or anger you've brought, the mountain is not appalled. It's seen and heard it all. It is one of the arms of God, where it is safe to lean awhile.

Kirkridge for many of us has been a thread in our lives. We have found safety here, rest here, acceptance here, love here. The founder John Oliver Nelson, who in 1942 had the vision to create a small band of brothers, soon to include sisters, committed to the renewal of the church. He found this place where Lenape Indians had roamed the hills and valleys, this place of beauty and wonder where the Spirit blows like the wind, hearts are warmed and when sometimes we are able, with Blake, "to see a world in a grain of sand / a heaven in a wildflower / to hold infinity in the palm of our hand/and eternity in an hour".

Today, Kirkridge is a thriving Retreat Center in the Poconos Mountains of Pennsylvania. They rent their facilities to groups like Tranquil Seas Retreat and also sponsor their own programs and retreats at the numerous facilities. We have enjoyed the accommodations at Nelson Lodge, Folly, Turning Point, The Farmhouse, Hermitage and Vanderbuilt. All have amazing views and fabulous meals prepared fresh each meal by the Kirkridge staff. The Kirkridge labyrinth is located within walking distance of the lodges and access to the Appalachian Trail is located within feet of Nelson Lodge.

Columcille, Inc. is a nonprofit organization established in 1978 to promote transformation through inner and outer work. It has its origins in Casa Colum ,Gaelic for Home of the Dove, a small house opened in 1975 by William Cohea Jr. as a 'salon by the side of the road' where 'tired sinners and reluctant saints' could drop by and share their experiences and ideas. Cohea had been inspired during a visit to the Isle of Iona to create an open space which welcomed people of all faiths and traditions interested in renewal and transformation. In partnership with Fred Lindkvist and "Friends of Columcille," the original foundation grew and Columcille erected the St. Columba Chapel in 1979. The building took its name from Colum Cille, the 6th century Irish monk who founded a monastic community on Iona.

Following construction of the chapel, the St. Oran Bell Tower was begun, patterned on eighth century Irish ruins. Shortly thereafter a stone circle was added, along with a small fresh water meditation pond. As more stones were set, the outlines of the present Megalith Park began to emerge. Today, Columcille includes the trilithon Thor's Gate, the Glen of the Temple, and numerous megaliths strategically placed on the land.

The unique spirit and inspiration of Columcille has been recognized by the National Museum of Art at the Smithsonian Institution, which includes it in its catalogue of cultural heritage sites. On June 21, 1997, the park was placed in conservation easement with the Heritage Conservancy to ensure its preservation as a sacred space and outdoor sanctuary. As a non-profit organization, Columcille is financed through the donations of visitors and friends and the generous support of its Members.

Megaliths

We frequently take our group to Columcille Megalith Park in Eastern Pennsylvania. Megaliths are giant stone structures placed artistically throughout a wooded mountain landscape that opens into lush green rolling hills and open spaces. I have never traveled to Stonehenge, but was reminded of it immediately. I had unknowingly stepped into a sort of ancient, spiritual landscape. I found that our group of chatty women had suddenly become very quiet and reverent as we walked the grounds of this park. It seemed to inspire an inner stillness, wonder and contemplation.

Many of the women on this particular retreat had studied Reiki. We could not help but feel an overwhelming energy from the stone structures. Even the greatest skeptics were seen holding their hands over the stones and connecting with this energy. Places such as Columcille always seem to redirect me to the experience that I am connected to something so much larger than myself. Daily problems that can seem so encompassing melt away next to a stone that has existed for thousands of years and will continue to exist for thousands of years after I am long gone. Part of the inspiration for Columcille comes from the legend of St. Oran, whose last words were, "The way you think it is may not be the way it is at all (Columcille, Inc., 2011)." This is a very fitting reminder in a landscape that invites us to press the boundaries of our habitual ways of thinking.

The word, megalith, literally means "large rock" and is Greek in origin. Most of the structures at Columcille are Polylithic dolmens which are free standing chambers of standing stones covered by a cap serving as a lid. Dolmens were used for burial and covered by mounds of earth. The monolithic type is called a Menhir, or large single upright standing stone. The inspiration for the megalith park at Columcille, is the island of Iona off the

Scottish Coast (Columcille, Inc., 2011). Consisting of four billion year old stone, this island has been a pilgrimage site of spiritual awakening for centuries. "According to Hebridean legends and oral history, early Celts saw Iona as a 'thin place' where one's spirit could travel through the veils that separate the worlds (Columcille, Inc., 2011)."

As architectural structures, megaliths are a source of wonder. They are among the earliest surviving structures in human history and we can only speculate as to their original purpose. They have been used, reused and modified for centuries by many different civilizations. Among some of the known usages of these sites are: astronomical observation, religious or ritual meeting places, burial sites and shrines.

Sources:

Columcille, Inc. (2011). Retrieved from Columcille Megalith Park: http://www.columcille.org/index.html

Hirst, K. (2011). About.com, Archaeology. Retrieved from Megalithic monuments: What is a megalithic sturcture?: http://archaeology.about.com/od/mterms/qt/megalithic.htm

Good Thoughts

Scientists have recently discovered mirror neurons. As we change our brain functioning through awareness, we change the energy of the brain and how information is transferred. This is an example of the mind/body/spirit connection. It builds an argument for neurological concept of prayer, wishful thinking and attunement.

The nature of our thoughts set intention.

MRI's have shown that the human inferior frontal cortex is active when the person performs an action and also when the person sees another individual performing an action. A mirror neuron is a neuron that fires both when a person acts and when the person observes the same action performed by another. So, the neuron mirrors the behavior of the other, as though the observer was itself acting. Therefore, I now include include a visualization of action or sometimes an actual visualization on a DVD during my guided meditations.

Guided Meditation

The following guided meditations are intended to be read aloud to an individual or group by a Facilitator.

Lie down on your towel or yoga mat and find a happy place.

Tune out the outside world and draw senses inward by bringing attention to the breath. Scan the body.

Detach from their thoughts and from negativity.

You are not your thoughts, but a calm presence.

When the meditation is over, lie in silence for a few minutes.

Meditation 1: The Sea

Prepare for the meditation by getting comfortable. Wear clothes that are easy to rest in and feel just right. Sit up with your feet touching the floor or lie down flat on a yoga mat.

Start by crossing your arms so your hands are resting on the front of your shoulders. This hand position means victory over ignorance, hate and violence. Set your intention for good thoughts, good words, good deeds.

Get still.

Now, place your hands and arms in a comfortable position. Close your eyes and take three deep breaths and begin.

The sound of the waves crashing against the jetty precedes the sight of the sea. Walking through the dunes, you can hear and smell the ocean before your feet touch the sand and you place your chair in the perfect position. Open the chair and drop your towel. Spread the beach blanket down on the warm white east coast sand. On this day it seems as white as salt. As you sit and get comfortable look up at the gorgeous white cumulus clouds in the perfectly powder blue sky. They are fluffy like cotton and inform us the sun will shine all day.

The sun's rays permeate the organs of your body and hit every inch of exposed skin. Feel the warmth. Feel the power of the Vitamin D you absorb and its healing energy.

The waves continue to crash creating white caps as high as the boardwalk. The pounding of those waves creates both an excitement and anticipation of becoming one with the sea. Reach for your boogie board now and get up from your chair and start walking toward the sea. Walk faster and then a little faster. Now run at top speed the way you did as a small child knowing you were safe and loved by the family and friends who took you to the beach. Run into the sea kicking past the small white caps and jumping them crashing into the waves head on. Place your body on the board in preparation for the ride in. Turn you head just enough to see the perfect curl of the wave that will carry you all the way in to shore.

You feel as if you are floating now as you ride the surf with not a care in the world. No past. No future. Just right now in the present and the closest you will come to levitating.

Standing up after that wonderful ride pick up the board and charge back in repeating that first with the boogie board and then getting adventuresome and body surfing in many more waves until your body feels fully alive with a tranquility that you set as your intention.

Walk softly back to your beach towel and place your body flat down with your eyes closed and resting in a yoga-like Savassana.

Think of nothing, just feel.

Feel the joy of knowing you are safe and loved and happy in your choices.

Feel the sun again to work its miracle, natures healing rays. Smell the fish and ocean scents. Taste the salt on your lips.

Listen to the sounds of the waves moving in and out with the flow of the tides and believe that this is the moment you need to take with you back into the world where we live our lives.

Knowing that you have the power to master tranquility.

Meditation 2: The Mountains

Prepare for a meditative journey high above the Blue Ridge mountains where the lenticular clouds hover like a massive dome over the Kittatinny range.

Calm your body and refocus your mind lie face up with your hands and legs relaxed and your head and neck on a pillow.

Focus on your breath, only the breath, let thoughts go. Inhale, exhale...inhale, exhale....inhale, exhale....inhale and hold it.

5, 4, 3, 2, 1.

Now exhale.

Your body is releasing tension. Feel your jaw relax and your shoulders sink down into the mat, your legs feel as if you are floating. Inhale cool air and fill your body. Exhale the tense hot air you have been holding.

Your body is totally relaxed.

Replace negative thoughts with positive affirmations. Set your intention to climb up and out of your stressful existence.

Visualize yourself floating on a soft white cumulous cloud. It is cotton like and puffy and looks like cauliflower. It is the fair weather cloud and a nice place to be. Living our lives in calmness and fair weather. Visualizing the serenity of equanimity and loving kindness. Hold on to your cloud and be safe, protected from all the ups and downs that the pressures of life toss at us. Hold on and experience the tranquility of your ride as a place you want to be in this lifetime.

You are rising up now as your cloud moves higher relaxed and resting with your arms and legs stretched out and floating. Look at the panoramic view of the mountain range. Looking up to see the nimbus and cirrus clouds. The gray covering that appears to be curling locks of hair almost in ringlets is misting with a slight drizzle.

As in life when we are faced with the fog we hold tight to our fair weather cloud and move forward. Now in view the rain snow sleet and hail from a dark nimbus high above the horizon but it passes quickly if we maintain the evenness of equanimity. We visualize ourselves holding our place on the fair weather cloud and break through the storms to the majestic view of the snow-capped mountain range. Open your heart and eyes to nature's beauty.

Enjoy the ride with gratitude for the ability to see and feel and smell the wondrous sights of a magnificent mountain range. Gratitude for what we do have. Gratitude for our good health and love of family and friends.

Ride down now on your tranquil cloud to the bottom of the mountain to a calming visual of resting near a beautiful stream that is filled by the snow running off the mountain. Feel the safety of the ground beneath you and knowing you are firmly grounded to earth's magnetic core. Grounded, in survival skills that serve you in life in the day to day trials and tribulations. Grounded in your ability to maintain balance in the face of any adversity.

Begin to slowly stretch as you sit up to take a last look at the serene stream flowing gently past your feet.

Move your fingers and wiggle your toes. Open your eyes and breathe deeply.

From the seated position rise slowly and stand tall.

Raise your hands up toward the mountain toward the sky.

Communication Skills

Passing The Talking Piece

The precursor to Tranquil Seas Retreat was Infinity Masters Circle – a group of women meeting weekly to learn new concepts and techniques in the hopes of improving quality of life and to share joys and sorrows. The use of a Circle was agreed upon as a fair and equal forum for discussion groups. The Circle is interactive and egalitarian. It enhances communication skills with a structure and nearly eliminates the stress produced by speaking publicly. No one has an obligation to speak if they don't want to. They can defer to the person sitting next to her/him.

The Talking Stick – sometimes called a "speaker's staff" or a "talking piece" is an object that promotes democracy during a discussion. In a tribal council circle, a talking stick is passed around from member to member allowing only the person holding the stick to speak. This permits all those present at a council meeting to be heard, especially those who tend to be introverted. Talking "lean" precludes the people who talk on forever from dominating the discussion.

✍**Illustrative Journal: by Janice P.**
Imagine a group of a hundred or so people in a large room sitting six or eight persons to a table, a buzz of chatter fills the air. A

very well-groomed petite woman enters the room donning a dark blue blazer donning a "RL" logo on the breast pocket. She has something in her hand, a smallish stick approximately thirteen inches in length that has a few ornaments on it, feathers, beads, crystals. She calls all the attention of the room to this stick and introduces it and herself to the room. The woman is Nora, a good looking woman whose strong presence easily takes command of the room. She states that she is the owner and a corporate director of several small companies. Some in the past, others she presently owns. She carries herself with confidence across the room engaging each one of us in the room, while still holding the stick in hand with great admiration.

The stick is a "Talking Stick" she instructs us used by Native Americans. The room grows still, then silent. She is easy to listen to. The Talking Stick has been used in large corporations such as Exxon she continues…its use? This "Talking Stick" allows both space and time for the person holding the stick to make a point, to have their say, to be heard. Ah, now she has our attention.

We all loved to be heard, these thoughts are apparent on our faces. Nora continues, there is more, it is not JUST a talking stick, there is a flip side, it is also a listening stick for all those in its presence at a meeting, or "Calling the Circle" as we come to learn. There are some additional rules, like time limits. We need to "talk lean", get to the point, be both quick and concise, but we also need to be attentive and open to the person who is holding that stick. Well, how does this process work then?

Nora then visits table by table, coaching us and providing topics for us to try it on for size. One by one, we try or take a "Pass" not wishing to add anything at the time and pass the stick to the person next to us in clock-wise order. We sit in our small circles, holding the stick, looking at it, turning it and feeling it in our hands, learning to compose our thoughts before talking, is there a bit of magic here?

We begin to speak, slowly, quietly, concisely with the refined words well thought out and pared down to the bone. The others at the table without the Talking Stick are clearly present and perhaps for the first time, listening to the words being provided by another person talking. They are learning NOT to think of what to say in response or what we wish to add to the topic at hand. Not always easy, but we are getting it, learning to speak, learning to be quiet, learning to listen…to really listen, to another's point of view. Nora has completed her teaching for the evening. Some of us take this message and use it at home with our family and friends, or to our co-workers in the office, others leave it at the table, but we are forever changed, for that moment in time and in the future.

Flash forward some three years. A small group of women together at a women's Tranquil Seas Retreat. Some of these women have known each other for ten years or more, others from the first time Nora has introduced the Talking Stick three years ago, still others have met for the first time today. The Talking Stick is introduced to everyone as it has been in the past. We all take it in, listen, learn new information or reinforce fragments that we have managed to keep since the last time we've done this. We keep our ears, eyes and hearts wide open. The Circle is called and we begin.

The topic: "What scares you past or present?" Honesty has entered the room with tears quickly on its heel. Empathy, a few open hearts, support, and compassion quickly arrive; in the end, encouragement and friendship remain. This transition has stemmed from those few lean words of the person talking holding that small unassuming but very powerful tool, and the open hearts and attention of those listening to those words provided. The Circle has done its job once more.

The Circle
During each Tranquil Seas Retreat we move into circle and set our intention to share openly and honestly in a confidential environment. We set the tone after a chakra opening session that

might include Reiki or Yoga. Speaking our truth with closed throat and heart chakra is more difficult.

The chairs are arranged in a circle and if it is a very large group, then into several circles. All participants can look into the eyes of the people in the room while they are talking. There is no leader once the circle has begun. The retreat staff explain the style, which we keep simple. First, the intention is set to explore a specific topic – so rather than "how is everyone doing?" it might be more like, "What is the one thing that has been on your mind this week about your relationships with other people?" Then, we teach it is imperative that we listen to each other so it is suggested that no one formulates what they plan to say while another is speaking. The style is extemporaneous speaking. Time limits are used as guidelines so that one person does not dominate the entire session.

✎Illustrative Journal: by S.R.

"Calling the Circle" is a unique way of communicating which most of us had never used before. When I first heard it described, I felt a tinge of discomfort..."I'm not going to be comfortable sharing intimate parts of my life with women I just met," I thought. I'm a fairly private person. I don't discuss my personal relationships with co-workers or casual friends. And I was reminded of situations in a corporate setting, where the facilitator has used similar techniques to get the participants to bond by sharing embarrassing moments or funny stories. I have really been uncomfortable doing that. But this technique is not what I have experienced anywhere else.

I'm what I used to call a shy person, recently I have discovered it's that I'm more sensitive than shy. I can go to a large event, weekend retreat or party and leave...never having met anyone new. I feel uneasy with people I don't know. So the idea of having to have everyone in the room focused on me, and having to be spontaneous...well, that was un-nerving at first. But I have found that "Calling the Circle" is one of my favorite parts of the Tranquil Seas Retreats.

I have been really working on becoming a better listener. Focusing on what the speaker with the stick is saying instead of desperately trying to come up with the most clever thing to say myself helps us to listen with more compassion, more empathy and to really understand what is being said. I have also found that the spontaneous response is refreshing to the speaker as well as the listeners. Sometimes what I have to say is still clever. Sometimes not so much. But that's not as important as I once thought it to be. If what I say is not clever and impressive...so what? No one is as judgmental as I feared they might be. And some thoughts seem to be clarified as we speak them when using this technique. But the most impressive thing about "Calling the Circle" is the connections that are made by merely listening with our hearts, as others share their thoughts, experiences, philosophies, joys, fears. Something quite magical happens, most of the time during the session. Women bond in a most special way.

One session during a smaller retreat was quite memorable…it was later at night and the group was small. There were seven women in the room. Some of us knew each other quite well. A few were new to the group, but friendly with others in the room. As the stick was passed, the subject of domestic violence came up. And as six of the seven women tearfully revealed their stories, there was not a dry eye in the room. All six had been afraid for their lives for a long time before leaving an abusive man. Each told a different story of how the man in their life, husband or long-term boyfriend, had threatened them. Each had a story of a gun being used to scare them into staying with the man. Each told of being certain the man they loved would soon kill them. The stories were each a little different. But the fear, the raw emotion brought up was the same. Each had been controlled by very similar behaviors on part of the man. Each had been emotionally abused and beaten down, still bearing the scars of that insecurity. Each still was a little afraid of getting out of their car in the dark. Some worried the man might someday show up to hurt them. The group put away the stick, and began a discussion which lasted long into the night.

Those women still think of that night when they hear of women who suffer domestic violence. And all seven feel sisterhood with all abused women…because of that night. We learned that we would never really BE alone again…we had always had sisters, wanting to help us, understanding our fears, waiting to stand with us, support us…we just hadn't known that at the time of the abuse. But that night those seven women cried together and loved each other and knew we would always be connected.

Why a circle?

After years of college and graduate school classes where the only thing I saw was the back of another student's head or maybe the tiny silhouette of a professor way down there in the lecture hall, I knew there had to be a better way. It wasn't until I lived in California that I was exposed to the benefits of a circle and being able to see the person who was speaking. My research took me to the 12th Century, to the culture of Indigenous people called Haudenosaunee who lived around 1142 C.E.

The Haudenosaunee people of the longhouse came from six tribes: Seneca, Onondaga, Oneida, Cayuga, Mohawk and Tuscarora. They meet in a Grand Council Circle and after lighting their fire exchanged ideas and opinions and formed a democratic government. In addition to the Swiss and Icelandic cultures, it is one of the oldest democracies. The study of this

Iroquois Society reveals that women gained a huge role in government thru the use of the Grand Council. Women existed as equal partners and owned property, horses, homes and farms. When the man entered into marriage he lived with the woman's family. The wife was totally responsible for the children and if the rare divorce did happen she got the children and the husband simply was asked to leave with his belongings. How civilized, this culture that existed so many years ago. All ties of the children were traced through the mother's family lines. The Chief's sister even selected the next chief. The female circle used men as runners between council and had the power to demote warriors and take away their symbol of power, the antler headpiece. They were even able to stop the men from going to war by voting against it. How did this happen? Simply put, the Grand Council, where seventy-five percent of the men and the women had to agree, created communication skills between civilized groups of people, facing each other in an open circle with a fire in the middle. We have much to learn from history!

✍Illustrative Journal: by T. I.

The power and support of women, together. Finally ready to decide to leave the man who had been a pseudo-husband for 5 years, very afraid... hearing the others in that small group share horror stories of men who had hurt them was very powerful.... at the end, Nora said, "we can all be grateful we are on the other side of this now," and looked at me..."even you..." I cried, finally accepting the truth that it was over with him. This moment gave me the strength I needed to get through the long break-up, becoming liberated, finally strong in my decision... more joyful! Free to be me, to emerge from the chrysalis our relationship had been, but that was a time to shed. Cutting etheric cords with a white-handled knife some months later didn't hurt either... And of course Reiki has been life-changing, a journey, begun on retreat with that first intense rush of hot-flash burning through my body. My first Reiki session, with Nora, before the attunement of course...learning that my root chakra was closed made so much sense to me. This understanding has helped me very much to understand what I had to do to exist safely and strongly in the world.

"Calling The Circle"

The term "Calling The Circle" originated with Christina Baldwin in her 1998 book of the same name. The use of a talking piece in combination with a circle of group interaction has been an indispensable addition to all Tranquil Seas Retreats. It is frequently mentioned by participants as the most emotionally liberating event of the weekend. This ancient practice establishes itself in modern day because of the ever increasing need for better face-to-face communication. It is imperative that we don't let email and text-messaging deprive us of our basic human need for true socialization.

__Yoga__

Flexibility of Body & Mind

Forms of mind/body exercise such as Yoga integrate mind and body with a sense of spirituality and connection with nature. They can be performed at lower intensities inclusive of a wide range of functional abilities, require no equipment and can be performed at home. The meditative awareness component involved can make this type of activity a complement to a meditation or an alternative to meditation for those who prefer higher levels of activity when trying to focus the mind.

Mind/Body Exercise

Yoga is a union between the mind and body. The six branches of yoga – Inana, Karma, Mantra, Tantra, Raja, Hatha – all have origins in Hindu spirituality. One branch, Hatha, has spawned several variations of what we have commonly come to know in the Western Hemisphere as yoga practice. The postures (Asanas) involve many physical movements such as bending and twisting, performed standing, seated, or lying on the floor. Combined with controlled breathing and meditative awareness, these movements challenge balance, flexibility, and muscular endurance. Yogic breathing Pranayama is used in conjunction with each posture to promote further connection between mind and body.

In is customary for the weekend classes at Tranquil Seas Retreats to both begin and end with Yoga.

The Friday afternoon Yoga practice is an effective way for retreat participants to relax and prepare for the reflective activities of the weekend. Saturday, more intensive Yoga workshops are offered to advance knowledge of the art and introduce even experienced practitioners to new avenues. Finally, classes conclude with a series of floor postures on Sunday that are designed to ground and center everyone as they prepare to return to daily life and use their newly acquired knowledge to find stillness in the whirlwind.

A Highly Customizable Practice

Considering that high-level professional athletes like NBA star LeBron James and tennis player Andy Murray practice yoga as part of their training, then it stands to reason that its practice can be valuable to you as well, considering the bevy of potential benefits it presents. Whether the objective is relaxation, muscle toning, spiritual evolution, or simply flexibility, a yoga practice can be customized to fit the needs of just about anyone.

✒ Illustrative Journal: by Maya Kowalcyk, Yoga Instructor

The first time I did yoga I was seventeen and had just enrolled as a dance student at the University of the Arts in Philadelphia, PA. I didn't know anyone. I had given up two years of English and Education studies at a prestigious college in Allentown, PA, to follow my dream of being a modern dancer on a stage. Aside from writing, movement makes the most sense to me. When I move my body, everything else seems to fall into place. I feel connected. I feel like I fit in, like this is what I am meant to be doing. One of the classes on the schedule that all dancers had to take was Yoga & Pilates. I had no clue as to what Yoga entailed and just figured that it would be another fitness-type class that would help me stretch and get stronger as a dancer. When the instructor walked into the class, I realized that I had seen her earlier that day, riding her bike up to the front of one of the other school buildings on busy Broad Street in Philly. When I watched her hook her bike up to the bike rack I was struck by how "in shape" she was. This girl, or woman, she seemed so young, yet more mature, to me, wasn't thin. You wouldn't call her svelte or waif-like, which is the image that many current yoga magazines portray as yoga teachers. This woman was simply – strong. She looked like she could take on the toughest gangster in town and come out of the brawl with a back handspring, somersault and then glide away on her bicycle. Well, of course, I didn't think of the back handspring part until after I saw her do yoga, but that was her.

Jenny - we'll call her that - didn't look like your average, toothpick, snap-you-in-half-with-my-two-fingers, ballet dancer, which is how most dancers are expected to look. In fact, one of our teachers at UARTS would walk around as we practiced at the barre and pinch us wherever there was room to pinch as he called out, "You need to eat more salads...YOU need to eat more salads...and you..." Teachers there weren't exactly focused on healthy body image. Their goal was to get you into tip-top shape to be the best dancer you could possibly be. The size of your thighs played a big part of being that dancer. Jenny didn't have the perfect dancer figure, but she intrigued me nonetheless. To this day, an image of her is imprinted on my mind. I only had that one class with her, and I never realized how much I would think of this instructor for the rest of my life, as the first person who introduced me to yoga. We never realize how important someone is until later in life. I wish I could remember her full name and write her a letter to thank her for just being that teacher. There were many other teachers after Jenny, but we always remember our first.

I did yoga off and on from 1997 to 2004. Then I started running long distance. I was fine while I was running three or fewer miles. When I started to run farther, my knees began to hurt. So, I began researching how to alleviate knee pain from running and read that yoga stretches might help. I started doing yoga before and after (sometimes during) each run and I actually noticed a difference. The pain was MUCH less. I integrated poses like Virasana (Hero's Pose), Supta Virasana (Reclining Hero's Pose), Crescent Lunge, Eka Pada Raja Kapotasana (One-Legged King Pigeon), Triang Mukaikapada Pascimottanasana (TMP - Three-footed Pose), Baddha Konasana (Cobbler's Pose), and Janu Sirsasana (Head-to-knee Pose). My painful knee actually was the catalyst that started me doing a regular home yoga practice. Before this time, I flitted from yoga class to yoga DVD to yoga TV program, without doing much of a home practice. My knee motivated me to research and see that certain yoga poses could alleviate certain types of pain. Yoga became medicinal, not just a hip way to stay in shape.

With yoga infused into my routine, I began running more and more and eventually completed a number of half-marathons. As my running progressed, so did my interest in yoga. I signed up for a teacher training at the Yoga Loft of Bethlehem and graduated in 2008. This in-depth study of yoga and all of its many parts, furthered my intrigue in the subject. To my surprise, one of my favorite aspects of the training were the discussions on Yoga philosophy, the Yamas and Niyamas, the other aspects of yoga that most of the Western world isn't aware of, or at least doesn't hold in the same esteem as they do the asana portion of the study of Yoga. My background in English literature and writing, with its emphasis on theory, on thought, seemed to have prepared me well for deep, life-pondering sessions in which we would relate yoga sutras to experiences in our own lives. At the end of the training, I felt like a child who had just learned how to read and looked forward to reading and discussing more about Yoga.

About the same time that I graduated from yoga teacher training, I was discussing yoga with a dear friend and co-worker of mine. I was a part-time waitress at the same restaurant that he was head chef for. He mentioned that yoga classes were hard to come by in this area. I myself traveled the 45 minutes to Bethlehem or Allentown, PA, to attend a class from talented and experienced instructors. John said, "You should start a class here, in Jim Thorpe," and then my mind began spinning. I taught my first class in Jim Thorpe at Flow Restaurant and Gallery (at the same location I waitressed for that short time), on a beautiful, hardwood floor, the walls filled with colorful and imaginative paintings by a local artist. A baby grand piano sat in the back of the room, and the artist's daughter would often come in at the end of one of our classes and play, more beautifully than seemed possible for a child of merely 7 or 8 years.

I taught yoga part-time for the next few years, at the art gallery, then at the Marion Hose Company, an old-fashioned fire house adjacent to the Mauch Chunk Opera House in Jim Thorpe. Then, when the hose company was sold to a city-goer who built sound equipment for notable musicians, the Opera House itself opened its doors to me. For the next couple years, I taught yoga in the upstairs lobby of the historical opera house, while I worked as a full-time high school English teacher. I stored my ever-growing supply of yoga props (blocks, blankets, belts, and mats) in the rarely used kitchen, and would move the necessary furniture out of the practice space before the start of each class. Students wrote their names on a paper sign-in sheet and put their money, ten dollars per class, in an open basket on a table - honor system style. The room was carpeted, a dull, bluish-gray indoor/outdoor style that had undergone years of trampling and would give off musty, old smells, especially in the heat of the summer months. We layered up (hats pulled down over ears, even) in the wintertime, and had three large fans on full blast in the summer months when the small space became a sauna. Sweating profusely, we would joke about how detoxifying it was. Then, I rented space in an old Victorian building that was now a sort of dance studio that used to be a grocery store and butcher shop in the early part of the 20th century.

I also continued my regular home yoga practice, and read Light on Yoga by B.K.S. Iyengar on a regular basis, referring to the medical suggestions in the back of the book whenever I came across a student with a certain condition. The small amount of free time I had kept me from devoting too much time to studying more in depth, though I occasionally thought how nice it would be to be able to learn more, to study more, to practice more yoga. Being the main income of my household, keeping a well-paying full-time job was necessary, however disagreeable.

I was itchy, though. I had a feeling that I needed something more in my yoga practice that I need to find a teacher. I remembered a phrase that one of the teachers from my teacher training (Jessie Thompson) had uttered during our training as a suggestion of what to do next after the training was over: Find a teacher who speaks to you and from whom you can learn and grow. I never had a regular "teacher" before. All the yoga classes I attended did certainly have "teachers." Yet, I didn't call any of them MY teacher. So, I went looking where most of us look today when we want answers to various questions that plague us: the Internet. That is where I found Joan White, my teacher, and Holly Walck, my second teacher and Joan's student.

In the spring of 2012 I began taking classes with Joan, a 2-hour one way commute. After a class with Joan there is a peacefulness that settles over me, a remnant of the experience of learning from a gifted yogi and teacher, a warm, wise woman. I also began studying with Holly, who was only one hour away in Bethlehem, PA.

Three months later, my world fell apart. My mother, only 65, suddenly died of an unexpected heart attack. She did not have heart disease. She walked for 45 minutes each day. She was a vegan. She did not take a single pill for a single health issue. She was the healthiest person I knew. And she went from energetic and cheerful to dead and gone in less than a week's time.

I didn't want to do anything. Except Yoga.

I went to my regular yoga class with Holly, letting her know what happened. She understood why I wanted to be there - to be in my practice while the rest of the world crumbled around me. In my practice I felt that the universe made sense. It wasn't a logical thought, but more of a feeling of "rightness" or of "understanding." All other worldly events, conversations, people didn't seem to make sense after her death. Practicing yoga, though, made sense. It was like opening a doorway to another part of the universe. This may not make much sense to you, unless you've lost someone very dear to you, but Yoga was like a portal that took me closer to where I imagined my mother might be. Again, it was more of a feeling, an intuition, than an actual concrete thought.

The more I practiced yoga, the more yoga I wanted to practice. I practiced every day, I read my Yoga Sutra book. I signed up for Holly's Yoga Studies Program to learn more, to go deeper. I just wanted to immerse myself in the subject of yoga. So, when Jennifer (the girl who ran the dance studio) called me and asked me if I'd like to take over her lease in August of 2012, I felt natural saying "yes." I would open a yoga studio and devote myself to the study, practice, and teaching of yoga in this area that needed it so much. And then I quit my full-time high school teaching job.

I knew that I couldn't give the required energy that the studio needed to open and flourish and still teach full-time, with a 2-hour daily commute and planning lessons and grading papers every night. So, with a little bit of money from my mother, I decided she would be proud of my decision to open the studio and focus on yoga, for a year, at least.

It took almost three months of cleaning, painting, and lots of elbow grease to get the studio where I felt it needed to be in order to offer an environment that would be welcoming and warm. On the last Saturday of September, 2012, we opened with a Grand Opening celebration of a weekend of classes in yoga, meditation, kid's yoga, belly dance, and hoop dance. Then, I began teaching a packed schedule that included 12 weekly classes in addition to taking care of advertising, bookkeeping, cleaning, and managing the studio and other teachers. A few months later we added a massage studio in the back room and then added massage therapy to our offerings.

In addition, I attended one or two weekly yoga classes with Joan and/or Holly and I dedicated myself to the Iyengar style of yoga, the most authentic, true yoga that I have come across and a style that is beneficial for all types of people, young and old, healthy and injured. I attended an Iyengar yoga teacher training in February of 2013 with Dean and Rebecca Lerner, and continue to hone my teaching style to make it more effective and based on knowledge of the practice and study of yoga, including texts like Light on Yoga, The Yoga Sutras of Patanjali, The Bhagavad Gita, Yoga a Gem for Women, the Hatha Yoga Pradipika, Light on Pranayama, to name a few.

When I first began to practice yoga, I had no idea what kind of "style" of yoga I was doing or that there were, in fact, so many "styles" of yoga available. Now I am able to look back and say that the first class I ever took was actually a Yoga & Pilates class. Then, I practiced mostly from Patricia Walden and Rodney Yee DVDs, who are both Iyengar teachers (Rodney Yee was initially a certified Iyengar yoga teacher, before going off on his own. His style of yoga still puts a lot of attention on alignment and breath, which are both characteristics of Iyengar yoga.)

Then, at Allegheny College in Meadville, Pennsylvania, I took a class with a teacher whom I am sure is an Iyengar (certified or just inspired) teacher. Later, when my knees began to bother me,

I was practicing along with my television, with Steve Ross, the "happy" yogi, and Ashtanga yoga where I experienced "vinyasa flow" yoga. I then began going to Jessie Thompson in Bethlehem for alignment-based yoga classes. I later learned that Jessie practiced weekly in New Jersey with a certified Iyengar yoga teacher, and that she was on the path to become certified herself.

When I found Joan White and Holly Walck a few months before my mother passed away, I knew I had found my teachers. In my first class with Joan, I left feeling like I had just come out of a deep, yet wakeful, sleep. There was a groundedness that left me feeling rooted to the earth and a lightness that went down deep to the core of my being. I also learned that I was unable to sit properly, or do Adho Mukha Svanasana Downward Facing Dog, one of the most seemingly basic yoga poses that I had been practicing for years properly.

As I walked out of her class, thanking her profusely with tears welling up in my eyes, I was awestruck that no other teacher seemed to have noticed these alignment issues in my body before. That's when I realized the power of observation that is necessary in a good yoga teacher. Joan is adept at observing a yoga class, even with 20 students lined up in front of her. A student, thinking she is hiding in the back row, will never get away with improper form or unsafe alignment in Joan's class. She can spot a sagging abdomen from one hundred feet away, and she turned 70 years this past year, in 2013. Holly has that same keen awareness of her students, having studied years with Joan and Patricia Walden.

Iyengar yoga, named for the originator of this method – B.K.S. Iyengar – is a practice that is methodical in its attention to detail and is often described as "alignment based" yoga. Many have heard of teachers of this form of yoga as being rather strict, often hitting students during class. This is true, but not always. B.K.S. Iyengar is known as the "World's Foremost Teacher" for good reason. He demands excellence, both of himself and of his students. Why? Because yoga is a serious subject.

Not only is yoga a physical practice, which could cause injury if done improperly, but yoga is about more than simply twisting yourself into a pretzel. It is about waking up to your true inner nature, your divine self, as Iyengar yoga practitioners might call it. If it is necessary to raise one's voice, to use physical touch, to be a bit unorthodox in order to achieve that goal, then that is what is required. I liken this approach to parenting. There is hitting, or abusing, a child, and there is disciplining a child by swatting his behind so that the child learns not to touch a dangerous object like a stove. The latter is a work of love in which harsh methods might be required to save the child's life. Yoga is the same way.

We fall into our patterns easily – mental, emotional, and physical patterns. Our mind wanders to the errands we have to run on the way home from work: get butter and milk at grocery store, have to get gas in car, pick up dry cleaning for my honey. Or, we instantly feel jealous as soon as we see that beautiful waitress smile at our significant other. Or, we slouch in our chair, cross our legs and slump our shoulders as we work for hours on the computer (yes; this is me, too!). Yoga is about waking up from these automatic patterns. Yoga is about union, becoming aware of the natural, true union between myself and the universe. Seems a lot different than what you first thought of when you went to yoga, right? One way to achieve this union is through the physical practice of yoga asana, actual yoga poses.

Although there are many styles of yoga, yoga is still yoga. People in the western world might turn yoga into a thousand different "methods," "styles," in order to market it a different way, but almost all of these various styles is included in the Iyengar method of yoga. In Iyengar yoga, however, the student is the judge of his or her practice.

In the morning, or if one is feeling lethargic, doing many minutes of Surya Namaskar (Sun Salutations) and back bending postures like Ustrasana (Camel), Urdhva Dhanurasana (Full Wheel), and Salabhasana (Locust) are helpful and are what should be practiced that day. However, if you are ill, or overworked, or physically or mentally spent, then a different yoga practice would be best. You might do Supta Baddha Konasana (Reclining Cobbler's Pose), Supta Virasana (Reclining Hero's Pose), and some inversions like Sirsasana (Head Balance) and Salamba Sarvangasana (Supported Shoulderstand) to rejuvenate your body and mind. You might hear of Iyengar classes described as being yoga for every BODY for this reason.

It doesn't matter what your age, what your condition, you can do yoga. If a certain asana (pose) seems inaccessible to you, your teacher will show you which props to use (chairs, blankets, blocks, belts, and more) to adapt the posture for your body. On the other hand, props are also often use to deepen poses, to go further. This use of props is also another signature of Iyengar yoga. In some yoga classes, you might even see ropes on the wall for inversions and other "rope" poses.

After years of practicing Iyengar yoga and experiencing for myself the healing aspects of this practice, I am even more dedicated to B.K.S. Iyengar often referred to affectionately as Guruji, or teacher, and grateful to have been so lucky to have come across his teachings. It has helped me achieve better posture (I look back, horrified, at pictures just a few years ago where my shoulders are collapsing forward and my upper back has a slight forward curvature.) It has also helped me deal therapeutically with my own Sacro-iliac joint pain that refers down the back and outside of my left hip and leg and also caused severe pain in my left lower back. Iyengar yoga has helped me be of great assistance in helping other students who have injuries or other physical ailments. I am by no means an expert Iyengar yoga teacher (I am in the process of becoming certified), but I have many resources (Light on Life and other therapeutic books and websites on Iyengar yoga) that I suggest to my students and I also consult with my own teachers, Joan and Holly, when faced with a situation I don't feel qualified to address on my own.

Jim Thorpe Yoga center was opened with the hopes that I would help bring yoga and other healing modalities to our surrounding community. It has been and done so much more.

We have a weekly meditation community Sangha that meets on Sundays at 10am and practices seated and walking meditation. This group has grown into a close-knit, welcoming community who supports each other in their efforts to develop a regular meditation practice to help each one be happier and more peaceful as they walk through life.

Our yoga classes for all levels of experience (Beginner Yoga, Slow Yoga, and Yoga for Levels Introductory through 3) offer guided, detailed instruction by experienced and talented instructors on alignment in yoga asanas and Pranayama (breathing exercises). These classes, as well, have become more than simply strangers practicing together. We have gotten to know one another. This is a group where you feel welcome, a family of yoga practitioners who care about each other. Because yoga, again, is about more than just the physical practice. It is about connection, with yourself and with others, and you will find that connection at our center.

We also have massage therapy and Reiki energy work available and will soon include Tai Chi and Kundalini Yoga among our offerings. Last year we began hosting Yoga Detox retreats to the Cape May, NJ, to relax and renew with yoga, healthy Ayurvedic detox foods, and peaceful walks on the beach. As we grow as a community, inspiring each other to be healthier and happier, we will continue to redefine what that looks like. As life is ever-changing, so must Jim Thorpe Yoga evolve to meet the evolving needs of its community. We are happy to be here and look forward to more successful years of mindful, healing practices. More than 200 classical yoga poses and 14 types of pranayama have been systemized by B.K.S. Iyengar in the development of Iyengar Yoga. These poses have been structured and categorized so that a beginner to the practice of yoga can progress safely from basic postures to the advanced ones. Iyengar yoga learners gain strength, flexibility and increased sensitivity in this process.

There are various sitting and standing yoga poses that could be a part of an Iyengar Yoga routine. In the beginning, these poses should not be held for more than 5 seconds, eventually increasing up to 5 minutes for some poses.

Some of the common Iyengar Yoga Poses include –

Adho Mukha Svasana (The Downward Facing Dog Pose)
Adho Mukha Virasana (The Downward Facing Hero Pose)
Halasana (The Plough Pose)
Padangusthasana (The Hand To Big Toe Pose)
Parivritta Parsvakonasana (The Revolved Side Angle Pose)
Parsvakonasana (The Extended Side Angle Pose)
Paschimottasana (The Seated Forward Bend Pose)
Salambha Sirsasana (The Headstand Pose)
Sarvangasana (The Shoulder Stand)
Savasana (The Corpse Pose)
Supta Bandha Konasana (The Reclining Bound Ankle Pose)
Swastikasana (The Ankle Lock Pose)
Tadasana (The Mountain Pose)
Trikonasana (The Triangle Pose)
Uttanasana (The Standing Forward Bend Pose)
Utthita Parsvakonasana (The Extended Side Angle Pose)
Virasana I, II & III (The Warrior Pose I, II & III)

For a beginner to the Iyengar yoga method of practice, one should start practicing basic poses like the following. Do each pose 2 to 5 times on each side, alternating right and left. All of the standing asanas (poses) - the first four poses below - strengthen and stretch the legs, arms and trunk of the body. In Geeta Iyengar's Yoga in Action: Preliminary Course, she explains that by working the legs in these poses, practitioners are reaching the lumbar, sacrum and abdominal regions of the body. These asanas also correct deformity in the legs, relieve backaches, neck-sprains, reduce fat around the waist, hips and thighs, reduce acidity, release gas, remove heaviness and bloating sensations in the stomach. All of the vital organs of the body are stimulated and activated. In addition, standing asanas especially benefit women, improving the functioning of the reproductive system, preventing malfunctioning of the ovaries and strengthening the uterus. Pregnant women can do standing poses without worry, using support and props as needed. The seated asanas (Upavistha Sthiti) teach the spine to extend, along with the abdominal cavity. The last two asanas below are of this type. One learns to stretch the legs completely while lifting both sides of the spine, without collapsing.

1. **Utthita Trikonasana** *(Extended Triangle Pose)*
Stand with your feet together and arms at your sides. (This pose can be done with your back to a wall for extra support.) Step your feet wide apart and raise your arms to the sides at the level of your shoulders. Your ankles should be in line with your wrists. Bend your right knee a little to turn your right foot and leg out 90 degrees. Then, turn your left foot to the right a couple inches. Your right heel should line up with your left inner arch. Keep both legs straight and exhale while you stretch your torso to the right, leaning out over your right leg. Place your right hand on your right shin or ankle and extend your left arm up towards the ceiling, stacking left shoulder over right. Your entire body should

be in line with your right leg. Inhale to come out of the pose. Repeat on the left. This pose

2. **Utthita Parsvottonasana** *(Intense Side Stretch Pose)*
Use two yoga blocks or stand in front of a table for support. Stand with your feet together and arms at your sides. Keeping the hips facing forward, step the left foot back about 3.5 to 4 feet away from the right foot. Your right toes are pointing straight ahead and your left toes are angled out to the left slightly. Place hands on your hips. Inhale, lift your chest towards the ceiling and roll your shoulders back, opening your chest. Keeping this shape, exhale while you bend forward. You can place your hands on the table or a wall in front of you at this point for extra support. When your back is parallel to the ground, bring your hands to the blocks or the floor, keeping your spine concave. Continue to breathe smoothly, and roll the shoulders away from the floor. On an inhalation, press your feet into the ground to lift the chest and come up. Step your feet together and repeat on the left side.

3. **Prasarita Padottanasana** *(Standing Wide Leg Forward Bend)*
Use two blocks or stand in front of a table for support. Step your feet wide apart, 4 to 5 feet. Keeping the toes pointing straight ahead, bring the hands to the hips and press the thighs back as you lift your chest upwards. With an exhalation, keeping this concave spine, bend forward. Bring your hands to the blocks or the floor, but keep your spine concave. Continue to press the

thighs back and lift the chest and chin. Be sure to press the outer edges of the feet into your mat to keep from collapsing the inner ankles. Inhale to lift the chest and come up. Bend the knees and slowly step the feet back together.

4. **Uttanasana** *(Standing Forward Bend)*
Use yoga blocks or a table/wall in front of you for support. Stand with feet under your hips or slightly wider. Inhale and reach your arms over your head. Exhale as you bend forward, keeping your back flat and chest lifting. Once your back is parallel to the ground (or sooner if needed), bring your hands to the table, blocks or floor. Do not let your back round. Use as much support as you need to keep the spine extending.

5. **Dandasana** *(Staff Pose)*
Three stages…
Stage 1: Sit on one to three folded blankets, with your legs extended out in front of you. If your back rounds easily, sit on a higher support. Bring your hands behind your hips and press your fingertips into the blankets or floor to extend the sides of the waist upwards. Lift the chest, roll the shoulders back and down, and extend through the heels of your feet. Toes should be pointing up towards the ceiling.
Stage 2: Keeping everything in stage 2, inhale and extend your arms up towards the ceiling. Keep the thighs moving towards the ground as you lift your chest. Stay here for a few breaths.

Stage 3: From stage 2, exhale and catch your feet with your hands. Use a belt to reach your feet if needed. Keep the spine extending, concave. Continue to lift the chest and chin up. Stay here for a few breaths. Inhale to lift the chest and come up.

6. **Pascimottanasana** *(Intense Stretch to the West)*
Sit on one to three folded blankets, just as for Dandasana. Go through all three stages of Dandasana. Use a belt if you cannot reach your feet. On an exhalation, release the head, extending the crown of the head forward. As your elbows bend, lift them out to the sides so they are in line with your shoulders and your chest can remain open.

Maya Kowalcyk, *M.A., RYT-200 Yoga* is the owner of Jim Thorpe Yoga Center, in Jim Thorpe, PA. For more information about Maya and Jim Thorpe Yoga Center, visit her website at www.jimthorpeyoga.com

Acupuncture

Bringing Meridians Into Balance

Acupuncture is a form of Eastern medicine that is used to alleviate pain and other maladies through the insertion of small, disposable sterile needles into the patient's skin. Vital energy runs through the body via meridians and it is the aim of an acupuncture treatment to bring balance and harmony to this energy flow.

Based in large part on neurophysiological concepts, acupuncture stimulates anatomical points on the body with the intent of nervous system regulation, the release of endorphins and immune system cells. Studies have also linked acupuncture to the release of neurotransmitters and neurohormones, which affect parts of the central nervous system that regulate involuntary functions such as immune reactions.

Acupuncture, though practiced for centuries in China, began to gain popularity in the United States after a 1971 article in the New York Times by James Reston, which detailed his experience with Chinese acupuncturists helping to ease his post-surgical pain. Since then, acupuncture has become widely accepted as a complementary medical treatment, with the numbers of practitioners and patients growing immensely over the past few decades.

The following is an interview with Acupuncturist, Dr. George Bonner...

Q: What was the catalyst for your moving toward energy/acupuncture work?

Dr. Bonner: During my time as student in chiropractic school at the University of Bridgeport, I developed friendships with many of my other classmates who were also into forms of energy healing and modalities such a meditation, Reiki and yoga.

One colleague of mine, Dr. George Russell, was a yoga practitioner, and he interested me in reading a book called "Anatomy of the Spirit" by Carolyn Myss. That book changed the way I thought about how healing worked. Carolyn basically described the Chakra system, which I was unfamiliar with at the time. She had correlated the chakra system with the seven sacraments, with the Tree of Life, so she combined Jewish mysticism, Christian mysticism, with the healing arts of the chakras. In particular, she described each chakra and how it related to a person's emotions, different energies that each chakra attracted, where someone's problems may lie in stagnation of chakra energy and how it related to our dispositions of different art types that we depend upon. That was a really big influence on me.

Subsequently, I devoured anything else I could find on Carolyn Myss, any of her writings or works. It just seemed she was giving great information on energy work like the feminine aspect of the healing arts. I really took a liking to that because it seemed much more compassionate; it seemed to rely on things much different than regular Western medicine. She was a medical intuit at the time, and spoke about how she brought a lot of her medical cases into her work. It really created inter-dependency between all of the different healing systems the basis for me, and I thought of things in terms of the chakra system. About a year after I finished reading her books, we had a nurse practitioner named April Greenfield, who taught Reiki I and II to a few of us in the class.

Q: How did you proceed to prepare and educate to do energy work?

Dr. Bonner: As a Chiropractor, I did do some Reiki initially as my first form of energy work and it was a great combination. I was able to see some things with relating to helping people with headaches, gastrointestinal distress or problems initially with the Reiki. When I was working on patients, they would always talk about how much heat was coming out of my hands and how warm things felt, which was pretty impressive to me because it was something that I didn't have a sense of control over. It felt like it really made me attune my sense of intention to help people with my placing my hands on them.

As a Chiropractor, I didn't only do chiropractic adjustments, I also did a lot of soft tissue work in addition to that, so I felt that there was much more benefit because the Reiki was being added. The more I had my hands on people, the more I felt there was a much better rate of success with their treatments.

I truly believe that acupuncture is one of the strongest forms of energy work there is.

After graduating from chiropractic school, there was an acupuncture program that opened up in the City of Philadelphia that was taught by a doctor from Chinatown. This program was associated with a school in China, the Tianjin University of Traditional Chinese Medicine. I did a three year program in the City (Philadelphia), and an approximate six month internship at Tianjin University in China, where we worked with a couple of the hospitals and private clinics and practiced all of our needling and things of that nature in China, so that really made a big difference in my work.

After my internship at Tianjin University, I studied under Dr. John Amaro, D.C., who runs the International Academy of

Medical Acupuncture. He was a Chiropractor who originally was one of the first acupuncturists in the country. He taught a synthesis of different systems – not just Chinese medicine – but things more along the lines of very more energetic properties relating to chakras and using things like lasers and colored light in place of just placing needles in for acupuncture. The way he taught it was: if you wish to become a master acupuncturist, then you needed to find out and study and do what the master acupuncturists do. So, he was one to say to find a mentor, follow, listen and read the classic texts of acupuncture, but remember that acupuncture was a principle in and of itself and not just a technique; that you could stimulate acupuncture points with massage, or moxibustion, or light or laser, or sound waves. He promoted a lot of computerized software to measure meridians, the flow and strength of the meridians, and be able to detect which acupuncture meridians were out of balance or out of harmony with their normal readings. He definitely made a big impact with my thoughts on that.

I also studied under a Japanese master, Kiiko Matsumoto, who was probably the foremost Japanese acupuncturist in the country. She teaches the Harvard physicians acupuncture program. I had a chance to study under her for about a year doing an internship with her. Her acupuncture which is Japanese based is a lot different that Chinese medicine because it's more palpation feeling and eliciting reflexes relating to the organs and muscles. It was very powerful because her technique was very surgically precise. She did not use lots and lots of needles; you might go in for a session with her and get only three needles, but if you got three needles, each one of those had a specific reasoning and she was able to confirm the reason why she was able to use those points on you, too. She was a very powerful doctor.

In addition to that, when I was in China, I had a fascination with auricular acupuncture which is all of the acupoints in the ear relating to the body. I was able to find and study under Dr. Nader Soliman in Rockville, Maryland. He is a medical doctor, but he was also President of the American Academy of Medical Acupuncture. He teaches seminars on auricular medicine, which is a form of acupuncture relating to using electromagnetic frequencies to stimulate acupuncture points in the ear. His technique is based on a French doctor, Dr. Paul Nogier whose son, incidentally, will be coming to Johns Hopkins University soon for a three day seminar which I plan to be a part of. Dr. Soliman's technique is measuring a pulse rate known as the vascular autonomic signal, and using ear filters and placing ear filters next to the energetic waves of the ear. The pulse rate then responds with either a greater or lesser amplitude whether it's an insult to the nervous system, or something that the nervous system can benefit from. So with that, Dr. Soliman is able to stimulate the acupoints in the ear with the electromagnetic frequency to put it back into balance. In addition to that, he also utilizes and teaches homeopathic remedies to basically work in addition to the auricular medicine treatment. He combines the homeopathy with that for a much stronger benefit for the patient.

Q: Discuss your passion to become a Chinese Medicine doctor.

Dr. Bonner: Well, after I finished up chiropractic school, I was getting ready to graduate, there was a local newspaper and they were doing an acupuncture demonstration for the University. That was something the University was looking to add to its program as it was a college of acupuncture and oriental medicine study. I volunteered to become an acupuncture patient for the newspaper, and I felt like after the needle placement, (I wasn't being treated for anything specific), it was something that I definitely felt a difference in my energy levels. There was a sense of euphoria after the acupuncture treatment and it really awoke a sense of curiosity in me, like "what's this acupuncture all about?" I got a little bit of experience studying and learning a little bit about meridians with some of my martial arts training, and one of my first acupuncture masters was Dr. Amaro, who was one of the first acupuncturists in the country -- he began his acupuncture training when Richard Nixon was President. Dr. Amaro basically always considered acupuncture as the ultimate martial art and he had based it on the premise that acupuncture was a healing art and a life-saving art, and because of that, he thought it was the pinnacle of the martial arts techniques.

Q: How does acupuncture work? Explain the meridians and how the client responds.

Dr. Bonner: Acupuncture in a sense, is channels of energy that flow through the body. They run from head to toe. The body is divided up into about fourteen different major meridians, and each meridian or channel of energy is basically related to an internal organ. Each organ is also related to a specific energy of the body, an emotion of the body; it's also related to colors, it's also related to the time of the year, it's related to specific functions. Some of the meridians are paired with other meridians in a mother-and-son type of transition, where you could treat the mother to make the son stronger, or you could treat the son to make the mother weaker; it's all related to a five element theory in Chinese medicine in which the body is comprised of vital energy known as "Qi", and this Qi flows throughout the body and basically gives us our life force.

The major premise with acupuncture is that when there is a stagnation of energy then usually there is some kind of dysfunction with the organ or pain in the body. Each one of these meridians has multiple points. Some in particular have many, for example the bladder has about sixty-nine points on its meridian. **One side of the body is deemed the Yin side of the body, and one side is deemed the Yang side. One side of the body is deemed to control the flow of blood through the body, and the other side is used to control the Qi through the body.** So, you can use and manipulate these meridians to stimulate the flow of Qi and break up the stagnation and increase the flow of energy.

There is also something known as the eight extraordinary meridians. A lot of famous Qigong masters utilize these meridians to help stimulate the flow. They are basically like a circuit breaker in order to speed of the flow of Qi or speed up the stagnation to relieve it. A lot of the ancient Chinese texts always think of Qi meridians as a flowing river, flowing water through the body. **Each meridian has a point on its meridian that is associated with one of the five elements in Chinese medicine theory. These elements are wood, metal, earth, water and fire.** So, you can manipulate each meridian based on which of the five elements that you are going to treat. Additionally, in Chinese medicine we utilize the diagnosis of the tongue in which the internal organs are represented in different areas of the tongue and different shades of color as well. We also utilize the pulse system in which there are about 28 different pulses that are found on the wrist. Unlike Western medicine pulses, these pulses are shallow or deep, and they are related all internal organs on the body.

Q: Discuss your Reiki training and how it works in synergy with your bodywork as a Chiropractor.

Dr. Bonner: Initially, when I first studied Reiki in chiropractic school, I used it primarily on headache complaints and also for stomach issues. It seemed to have a very favorable influence. There were also times when I would use it on myself when I was feeling low on energy or just feeling that there were issues with myself relating to digestive problems as well. After a little while in practice as a Chiropractor and started becoming seeing more and more patients and heavy volume, I tended to get sort of away from the Reiki. It was almost like I would do Reiki as a stand-alone treatment instead of in conjunction with the chiropractic based on certain time constraints. Then altogether, I started getting more and more away from Reiki and just focusing just on the chiropractic and then the acupuncture. It was almost like it was dormant inside me and I just hadn't used it enough. I thought to myself 'hey, I have this other modality that can help people with and I'm not using it properly'. So that, in and of itself, caused me to start using Reiki more in addition to the soft-tissue work that I do as a Chiropractor. It definitely made a huge difference in the quality of the health and response in the treatment that the patients were receiving.

I recently had a massage therapist that I treated who was complaining about issues that I thought were related to her adrenal glands. Upon doing a Reiki treatment on her, we found that there were a lot of issues relating to her root chakra – her sacral chakra. She had reported some of the sensations she was feeling… almost like there was dripping water down the lower portion of her sacrum during her treatment. Subsequently, a few weeks after the treatment, she went in for an ultrasound and they did find out that she actually had a cyst in that location and she was getting some work done to have that removed. She came back to me and said that the Reiki treatment is what really triggered her to go and further investigate what was really going on in that area because I had told her that there was something going on in the root chakra. Based on her history and also what the energy of the Reiki treatment had directed me towards, I focused the majority of my treatment on there, and her response was almost like – it wasn't intuition, it was stronger than that, but it was the energetic connection signaling where there was dysfunction in this patient's body.

Q: How long has it been since you've been more active now incorporating chiropractic and Reiki together? You said that you had drifted away from it – when did you get back to it?

Dr. Bonner: The first five years in practice I was doing a lot of Reiki, and then I would say probably five or so years after that I really didn't do much with it. So, it's only been within the last year or so.

Q: What are your future plans for River Wards Wellness Center? How will you treat patients going forward?

Dr. Bonner: With River Wards, my main goal is to combine the best of functional medicine, the best of acupuncture, the best of chiropractic, the best of exercise therapy, and the best of energy work all under one roof. With that, we will have a synergistic effect on a patient. I want to be a game-changer in people's health. I also want to be a leader in holistic healing, combining all these with a teamwork style approach. I think people are going to come and get treatments that are going to be quantum leaps in their body's ability to heal itself. Basically, we're allowing the patients to heal themselves by giving them the opportunity to take away this Qi stagnation by freeing up the chakras, by improving the alignment of the spine and nervous system integrity, and also by improving nutritional status and the functional status of patients through their health care.

Dr. George Bonner, D.C. studied Acupuncture and Chinese Medicine at *Tianjin University of Traditional Chinese Medicine* in Tianjin, China. He is the Owner/Operator of River Ward Occupational Medicine & Wellness Center in Port Richmond, Philadelphia. Dr. Bonner can be contacted via email at drgeobonner@yahoo.com

Reiki

Harnessing Energy For Wellness

Reiki teachings state that there is a universal 'life force' energy, which can be accessed by practitioners to induce a healing effect. The belief is that energy will flow through the practitioner's hands whenever the hands are placed or held near a potential recipient. Some teachings stress the importance of the practitioner's intention or presence in this process, while others assert that the energy is drawn by the recipient's injury to activate or enhance the natural healing processes. A second level of training, including another initiation, is said to enable the practitioner to perform Reiki treatments from a distance. This method, it is stated, involves the use of special symbols to form a temporary connection between the practitioner and the recipient, regardless of location, and then to send the Reiki energy.

The energy involved in a Reiki treatment is said to be 'from the Universe,' rather than the personal energy of the practitioner, and is therefore inexhaustible. Reiki is described by adherents as a holistic therapy which brings about healing on physical, mental, emotional and spiritual levels. It is said that healing may occur in any or all of these domains in a single treatment, without any conscious direction needed by either the practitioner or the recipient. Reiki involves a touch of hands onto the body, allowing energy to flow freely through the Chakras.

What is a Chakra?

Chakras are spinning wheels emanating from nerves in the spinal column. The word "Chakra" originates from Sanskrit. There are seven that we learn in Reiki trainings that correlate to the endocrine system and to colors. If the chakras are open and clean spinning and we aren't losing any energy and disease processes are unable to permeate the etheric level and attack our body. All of the energy clearing activities at Tranquil Seas Retreat are designed to give people techniques to keep the chakras clean and open and spinning perfectly. The Qigong, Reiki and Yoga are excellent modalities for this purpose.

The root chakra is located in the area just below the waist and relates to the adrenal medulla and produces the flight vs fight response. All of the basic survival instincts come into play with this chakra. We feel there are ancestral memories imbedded in this chakra of trauma from our ancestors. The associated color is red.

The sacral chakra is located in the genital area and dominated by sexual hormones. It is about pleasure, reproduction, addictions and most significantly ability to accept abundance. Its color is orange.

The solar plexus is located in the stomach region and many physical problems from gall stones to ulcers are found in this area. It is also the seat of relationship issues and if the chakra is not spinning clean can include giving up power in relationship. Its color is yellow.

The heart chakra located in the chest is related to the thymus and the immune system. It is the seat of t cells which fight disease. The color is green and when this area is dirty spinning heart disease and poor circulation can result. Emotionally a break up can trigger an inability to love oneself and to be devoted to a compassionate life.

The throat chakra dictates growth and maturity and communication skills. It correlates to the thyroid and most importantly when open allows us to speak our truth. The color is blue.

The third eye chakra between the brow is dominated by the pineal gland, which produces melatonin and restful sleep. It is also the seat of intuitive ability and clairvoyance and open mindedness. The color is indigo.

The crown chakra correlates to the pituitary gland and is the seat of spirituality. I often teach that many religious leaders protect their crown chakra by wearing hats as with cardinals and rabbis. The color is purple.

The lower level chakras vibrate at slower speeds than the top Third Eye and Crown. If the throat chakra is blocked it is hard to have an open third eye. There are many interactions between the chakras such as both solar plexus and heart being dirty, closed or spinning off energy during a marital divorce.

The 7 Chakras

Crown Chakra
Connection: Spirituality
Anatomical Association: Pineal Gland
Color: Violet
Pitch: B

Third Eye Chakra
Connection: Perception
Anatomical Association: Pituitary Gland
Color: Indigo
Pitch: A

Throat Chakra

Connection: Communication
Anatomical Association: Thyroid Gland
Color: Blue
Pitch: G

Heart Chakra
Connection: Emotions
Anatomical Association: Thymus Gland
Color: Green
Pitch: F

Solar Plexus Chakra
Connection: Assimilation
Anatomical Association: Liver
Color: Yellow
Pitch: E

Sacral Chakra
Connection: Sexuality
Anatomical Association: Spleen
Color: Orange
Pitch: D

Root Chakra
Connection: Survival
Anatomical Association: Adrenal Glands

Color: Red
Pitch: C

Attunements

An attunement opens the body's energy channels and connects them to Universal Chi. The Reiki attunement is a procedure to open the energetic healing powers. It is performed by someone who has already been a healer for a long time called a Reiki Master. It is a wonderful ceremony training and empowering the new Reiki.

The teaching of Reiki is commonly divided into three levels, or degrees.

First degree: REIKI I
The first degree Reiki course teaches the basic theories and procedures of how to work with Reiki energy. The channel through which Reiki energy passes to the practitioner is said to be opened or widened through four "attunements" given to the student by the teacher. Students learn hand placement positions on the recipient's body that are thought to be most conducive to the healing process in a whole body treatment. Having completed the first degree course, the participant can treat himself and others with Reiki. The course duration is typically two days, although this varies widely.

Second degree: REIKI II

In the second degree Reiki course, the student learns the use of three symbols which are said to enhance the healing effect and allow for distance healing. Another attunement is given which is said to further increase the capacity for Reiki to flow through the student, as well as empowering the use of the symbols. Having completed the second level, the student can treat people with Reiki without being physically present with the recipient.

Master Level: REIKI III

Through the third degree, or "master training", the student becomes a Reiki Master. One or more attunements are carried out and the student learns a further master-level symbol. Having completed the master training, the new Reiki Master can attune other people to Reiki and teach the three degrees of Reiki. The first and second degrees are prerequisites for the master training. The duration of the master training can be anything from a day to a year or more, depending on the school and philosophy of the Reiki Master giving the training. In the case of comprehensive training, the third level is often broken into two or three smaller stages of attunements and teaching.

Healing occurs as we allow ourselves to be the conduit for the universal spiritual wisdom of Reiki. Reiki integrates into your whole being physically, emotionally, mentally and spiritually.

There are several obstacles which preclude this spiritual practice. Included in that list are hate, fear-based emotions, indecision, immaturity and arrogance.

Reiki principles serve as a structure to move past these obstacles. The principles are taken from affirmations.

Principles of Reiki
1. JUST FOR TODAY, DO NOT ANGER
2. JUST FOR TODAY, DO NOT WORRY
3. HONOR YOUR PARENTS, TEACHERS AND ELDERS
4. EARN YOUR LIVING HONESTLY
5. SHOW GRATITUDE TO ALL LIVING BEINGS

These principles or precepts are powerful guidelines to live by and goals to be achieved. If we learn not to anger we will be able to show gratitude. Showing gratitude to all living things will result in anger not being able to arise. It is imperative to practice what we say we believe. Healing the relationship with parents and elders is more about gaining insight into how those interactions have created imprints in our youth that to this day cause distress. When a person receives a Reiki treatment, the Reiki flows into the energy field affecting the Ki and it also goes around the organs. Create healthy imprints that come in the form of saying something, doing something or even thinking something positive. Worry shuts down the sacral chakra and stops abundance from flowing into your life. When you stop worrying, then abundance returns, because the thoughts that run through your head all day determine your emotional state.

✐Illustrative Journal: by Michele Wosak, Reiki Master

Adding Reiki to my life has been a wonderful learning experience that will always be with me. Losing two loving persons in my life in an eleven year span had taken its toll on me. I needed to find some peace, some comfort in my life, trying to reason out where my life was taking me. Thanks to some wonderful friends, I was introduced to Reiki. To be able to use my hands as a conduit to healing energies – wow! The feeling of peace and tranquility when practicing Reiki has had a profound effect on my life. Reiki treats the whole person, body, mind, spirit – opening up our chakras – allowing our energy to flow to where it is needed in our bodies – just amazing! Attaining my Master's certificate in both Usui and Karuna disciplines has allowed me to share the healing powers of Reiki with family, friends and clients. Working at Nora's retreats, no wonder they're called "Tranquil Seas", has given me a deeper appreciation of the healing power of Reiki. At one of our first retreats, we had five Reiki Masters in a large conference room giving Reiki treatments to the attendees. The energy in that room was amazing, each one of us connecting with our clients through Reiki – what a wonderful experience!

Chakra Clearing

When the Chakra system is out of balance we can't vibrate and function at our optimum. Remember if the Chakras are closed or dirty or spinning off energy, the body is at risk of disease permeating it. All illness starts first in the human energy field before manifesting in the physical body. A Reiki session using the diagnostics available to determine which chakras are out of balance is the most efficient way to proceed. A Reiki professional or yoga instructor has many techniques available to balance the energy. We elect to use a pendulum technique during our sessions. However, all participants are taught how to do this on themselves with a simple style of placing their hands on top of each other and going down their own chakra system. The Chakras can be cleared using one of the methods taught at Tranquil Seas Retreats:

First, placing hands together a little above the chakra, move your hands in a counter-clockwise fashion, drawing out the congestion. Next, go back in a clockwise direction with positive thoughts and the intention of clearing and balancing. Then move to the next chakra.

This simple technique done weekly helps the body to keep the wheels turning and permitting the energy to flow evenly.

Physical Exercise

Train Your Body To Function At Its Highest Level

Human beings are not suited to a sedentary lifestyle. Having evolved under conditions that required very intense physical activity, humans are built to have the ability to generate fast and powerful movements. Improvement of overall health, body composition, athletic performance, mood, and other benefits will be result of a properly performed fitness program.

Efficient Conditioning

Cardiorespiratory fitness and changes in body composition can both be achieved without marathon exercise sessions. While the "Aerobics" craze of the 1980's and subsequent spinoff programs were cleverly marketed, the notion that signing up for a class at the gym and then jumping up and down for and forty-five minutes as a necessary component of cardiovascular fitness is outdated. Beginning with studies conducted by Dr. Izumi Tabata on the subject of interval exercise, many people ranging from casual gym-goers to professional athletes have adopted brief, intense interval training to augment the more time consuming treadmill/jogging style methodologies of the past.

A typical interval training methodology would be to select a few exercises and perform each for twenty seconds, resting for ten seconds in between each exercise, then repeating the cycle seven times so the work is performed in a total of four minutes. For example, if you select push-ups and kettlebell swings as the exercises, first perform twenty seconds of push-ups, followed by a ten second rest. Then perform twenty seconds of kettlebell swings, followed by a ten second rest. Then continue the cycle. If desired, the first four minute circuit can be followed by more circuits, provided you have gradually worked up to that level of conditioning. If in doubt, do less rather than more, because over-training can result in counterproductive setbacks.

Resistance Training and Fat Loss

The production of lean muscle tissue has been shown to alter metabolic rate and greatly facilitate fat loss. Even a small change of adding five pounds of muscle to your physique while subtracting five pounds of fat will create a dramatic and visible change in appearance. A simple program of resistance training performed at high enough intensity levels can produce the type of results that will both efficiently improve aerobic capacity and improve aesthetic appearance. Training for strength at higher levels of intensity not only accomplishes desirable results regarding fat burning and overall conditioning, but it does so in a shorter period of time and a reduction in the type of repetitive stress injuries incurred as a result of low-intensity exercise such as jogging. An additional advantage is that resistance training can be performed indoors or outdoors, and with minimal equipment. Coupled with a brisk walk on alternate days, it makes for a fitness program that is enjoyable and beneficial for general well-being as it is productive in achieving goals of body composition change.

Bodyweight Exercises

Though it may not be practical or possible to make it to the gym four times a week, your own bodyweight is always available for use a fitness tool. It is equivalent to having a 24-hour gym anywhere you happen to find yourself. Properly progressive bodyweight exercises can help you build muscle, burn fat, or both. "Progressive" in this case simply means moving forward with progressively more difficult resistance by decreasing the amount of leverage available. For example, you might begin by doing standing push-ups against a wall. After you have developed your ability, move on to knee push-ups on the floor. Then progress to conventional push-ups. After that, try push-ups with your feet elevated on a chair. Finally, you'll be doing one-armed push-ups, just like Rocky.

When resistance is moved along to meet the development of your fitness level, your body adapts and improves. If you have doubts about the effectiveness of using primarily bodyweight as resistance, the answer is found in a cogent (yet potentially offensive to some) example: Consider the powerful physiques that convicts develop while incarcerated. The circumstances under which they are attained includes nutritional intakes that are lacking in protein, substandard (if any) weight training equipment, and very limited time and space to conduct the workouts. The unconventional methods they employ are directly converse to needlessly complicated workout protocols commonly found in fitness books and magazines that also espouse near intolerable levels of protein and expensive supplements. If you're uncomfortable contemplating the push-up/squat regimens utilized by inmates, a kinder and gentler analogy can be found in the incredibly lean and muscular physiques of gymnasts, usually built with only bodyweight exercises…primarily chin-ups and parallel bar dips. Next time you are watching the Olympic Games, notice that the core and shoulder development of male gymnasts is comparable to that of advanced bodybuilders. When making the comparison between those two groups, also consider that gymnasts accomplish their results without assistance from the massive quantities of steroids and growth hormones that are universally used by competitive bodybuilders. With this knowledge in hand, rest assured that a good progressive bodyweight exercise routine will allow you to achieve your fitness objectives naturally, and without any expensive equipment or gym memberships.

If you don't want to add muscle size, simple stay with the easier movements in higher rep ranges. For example, do push-ups against the wall in sets of 25 repetitions.

In general terms, the following repetition protocol can be used as a basic template…

If Your Goal Is:

Strength

Utilize movements that will allow you to perform between 3-8 repetitions. To gain strength, work your way progressively up through more difficult movements to the most challenging variation of its category (such as the one-arm push-up). Aim to complete 25-30 reps per session broken down into 5-10 sets. In other words, perform 5 sets of 5 reps. Or perform 10 sets of 3 reps. Either of those set/rep schemes will be optimal in achieving strength gains. Rest as long as necessary following a set to recover most of your strength before the next set (this is generally between 2 to 5 minutes).

Muscle Size

Utilize movements that will allow you to perform between 8-12 repetitions. To achieve larger muscle size, utilize a moderately difficult movement such as the conventional push up and perform 3-5 sets of 8-12 repetitions each. Slow down your rep speed to eliminate the use of momentum and keep the muscle under constant tension – something in the area of 1-2 seconds up and 1-3 seconds down will work. To keep the intensity high, reduce rest periods in between sets to 60-90 seconds.

Fat Burning / Endurance

Utilize movements that will allow you to perform between 15-50 repetitions. Lining up the exercises in what is called a "Circuit" is very useful when working towards muscular endurance. A circuit is a series of exercises that engage different muscles, performed continuously with little or no rest between movements. After completion of each series of exercises, a short rest may be taken before completing another circuit.

A sample circuit might look like:
Bench Squats – 15 reps
Crunches – 15 reps
Vertical Pulls – 30 reps
Leg Raises – 10 reps
Push-Ups – 10 reps

Ab Rollouts – 15 reps

Jump Rope – 2 minutes

2 minute rest, then repeat circuit

This style of exercise is very useful for fat burning because of the high level of activity involved. The intensity can serve to provide a shorter workout with greater benefits, as it taxes the cardiovascular system adequately without exhausting the muscles, mitigating muscle soreness and release of Cortisol. Work hard, but remember to work smart as well. Always ensure enough rest and proper nutritional intake of protein and complex carbohydrates to nourish the muscles and assist the body in recuperating.

A Few Tips…

* **Always be safe**. There will eventually come a time when the ability of the muscles exceeds the tolerance of the joints and tendons. Protect yourself by always using proper exercise form and technique, and by getting adequate rest and recovery.

* **Workout routines don't need to be complicated to be effective**. One upper body pulling movement (Chin-Up), one upper body pushing movement (Push-Up), and one leg press movement (Squat) is all that is necessary for a full body workout. If desired, you can add in a few specialization exercises for the abdominals, calves, or anything that suits your specific goals. Repeat your workout two or three times per week and get adequate rest and nutrition. It isn't unrealistic to say that with sufficient intensity, three 30-minute workout sessions each week could make a dramatic difference in appearance and physical performance.

* **Complete a brief 5-10 minute warm up prior to exercising**. Doing so will prepare the body for what is to follow – making the muscles more elastic, lubricating the joints, alerting the nervous system, and focusing the mind on its task. The amount of warm up necessary will vary on several factors, such as your age and the outside temperature, but a few easy high-rep movements or some light cardio is a good starting point. Basically, you want to do enough to get a light sweat going, but not so much that you wear yourself out before the real workout. Like everything else in life, you must determine the proper balance according to your individual situation.

* **Start slow, and progress slowly**. While training hard is important, utilizing proper progression takes patience and self-discipline. Don't rush into things like one-legged squats without taking the time to properly strengthen the muscles and connective tissue. Injuries acquired through improper training

will do nothing but hold you back. As such, complete your reps deliberately, always with proper form. Once you reach the last rep you can complete with good form, stop your set. Don't hang on the chin up bar flopping around and kicking your feet in the hopes of squeezing out an additional rep. Gyms are full of macho types who attempt to lift unreasonable poundage with improper form. Not only is this approach often risky, but it will, barring the use of performance enhancing drugs, usually effect an outcome of substandard results. Train smart, and you may be able to jump on a chin-up bar and complete more perfect reps than the muscle-head know-it-all who is eager to give you his bad advice on strength training.

* **Breathe. Never hold your breath**. A good rule of thumb is to exhale on the raising portion of any resistance movement and inhale on the lowering portion of any resistance movement. Holding your breath during resistance exercise can raise blood pressure to dangerous levels, so the important thing to remember is just to breathe no matter if you choose to take one breath per rep or two or three. Just make sure to keep the air flowing.

What follows is a sample weekly fitness program that can be performed at home with minimal equipment in less than 30 minutes a day:

Always consult your Physician before beginning any exercise program. The material in this book is for informational purposes only. The activities, physical and otherwise, described herein for informational purposes, may be too strenuous or dangerous for some people. As each individual situation is unique, you should use proper discretion, in consultation with a health care practitioner, before undertaking any exercises described in this book. The author and publisher expressly disclaim responsibility for any adverse effects that may result from the use or application of the information contained in this book. Stop exercising immediately if you develop chest pain, shortness of breath, lightheadedness or dizziness. Consult a qualified fitness professional for routines and exercises best suited to your goals and abilities.

Beginner Fitness Program

Day 1

5 minute warm-up: Jump Rope
* It is not necessary to jump rope for 5 minutes straight – just set a timer and complete as many reps as possible within the allotted time period, taking rest breaks as necessary. As your overall fitness level improves, shorten the breaks, then eliminate them completely as you become able to complete 5 consecutive

minutes. Shorts intervals work well for this purpose – for example, you could jump rope for 20 seconds, then rest for 10. Repeat until the 5 minutes time period is complete.

Supported Squats (30 total reps, split into 3-5 sets)
Because they activate more muscle than just about any other exercise and work the thighs and posterior (where much athletic power is generated), squats should be the foundation of any good fitness program. The supported squat is a variation used to progress to conventional parallel squats, utilizing a chair or other stable object to assist with balance and support. To perform it, stand with the feet shoulder width apart and extend the arms forward, holding on to the back of a chair or sturdy object that is at least waist high. Slowly bend at the hips and knees and lower yourself until the thighs are parallel with the floor. Keep your back straight without rounding, keep your heels flat on the floor and ensure your knees don't extend out past your toes, keeping the shins as vertical as possible. From parallel, push yourself back up using mostly power from your legs, with an assist from the chair if necessary.

Vertical Pulls (30 total reps, split into 3-5 sets)
Pull-ups (palms facing outward) and Chin-ups (palms facing towards you) are a great exercise to develop strength. Because they are amongst the more difficult bodyweight exercises, several preparatory steps may be necessary to work up to a full chin-up.

The vertical pull is a basic starting point. Simply stand in a doorway (or any sturdy object you can safely pull on) and get your toes about 3 to 6 inches away from the object you're holding on to. Take a strong grip and slowly lower your body backwards to about arm's length (or as far back as you can go if you are uncomfortable extending to arm's length). Then pull yourself back to upright by bending the arms in and keeping the shoulder blades tight.

Wall Push-ups (30 total reps, split into 3-5 sets)
Wall pushups can be done against the very same object you held on to for vertical pulls. Face the object or wall with your feet about arm's length away and extend your arms to the object/wall at chest level. Then bend your elbows and lean in very slowly until your forehead comes close to the wall. It is basically a vertical version of the same type of pushup you learned in grade school.

Side Bend Stretch *
Stand upright with feet shoulder width apart with arms at your sides. Raise your right arm over your head and bend to the left side, sliding the left hand down the side of your leg. Hold this position for 30 seconds, then repeat on the opposite side.

Forward Bend Stretch *

Stand upright with feet shoulder width apart. Bend forward at the hips and slide your hands as far down the legs as possible without excessively rounding the back. Pull yourself gently downwards and hold for 30 seconds.

Diamond Stretch *

Sit on the floor and bring the soles of your feet together, pulling them towards you so that your legs form a diamond shape. Drop your legs towards the floor to stretch the thighs and groin. Lean forward slightly, apply gentle pressure and hold for 60 seconds.

* A short yoga practice like the one found in the Yoga section of this book can be substituted for these stretches.

Day 2: Rest

Day 3

25 minute walk

Crunches (10 total reps)

Lie on your back and cross your hands over your chest (minimizing the chance of neck strain that can result from putting your hands behind your head). Very slowly and under control, lift your shoulders and core up towards the ceiling, crunching the ribcage toward the legs. Hold for a second at the top of the movement, then lower back down slowly.

Day 4: Rest

Repeat Cycle

Intermediate Fitness Program

Day 1

5 minute warm-up: Jump Rope

Squats (50 total reps, split into 5-10 sets)
Stand with the feet shoulder width apart and extend the arms forward, holding on to the back of a chair or other sturdy object that is at least waist high. Slowly bend at the hips and knees and lower yourself until the thighs are parallel with the floor. Keep your back straight without rounding. Keep your heels flat on the floor and shins as vertical as possible, ensuring your knees don't extend out past your toes. From parallel, push yourself back up using power from your legs.

Negative Only Pull-Ups (20 total reps, split into 5-10 sets)

Removable Chin/Pull-up bars that can be hung over the top of a doorway can be purchased at Walmart or any store that sells fitness equipment for about $30. Bars can also be found in just about any public park. Before you are able to perform conventional pull-ups, utilize negative repetitions by climbing up to the bar on a chair, holding yourself in the top position with your chin extended slightly past the bar and slowly, under control, lowering yourself down over a period of 3-10 seconds. Climb back to the top and repeat.

Push-ups (30 total reps, split into 3-5 sets)
Lie face down on the floor with your hands under your shoulders and your feet about shoulder width apart. Keeping the legs and core straight and tight, push yourself up until your arms are straight at the top. Pause at the top for a second, and then lower yourself down until your chest lightly touches the floor. The push up is rightfully regarded as the classic upper body conditioning exercise, and is a much more natural and safer movement than the bench press or most other varieties of pressing movements.

Side Bend Stretch
(refer to beginner workout program for description of stretches)

Forward Bend Stretch

Diamond Stretch

Day 2: Rest

Day 3

25 minute walk

Crunches (25 total reps, split into 3-5 sets)
(refer to beginner workout program for description)

Leg Raises (10 total reps, split into 1-2 sets)
Lay with your back against the floor, legs extended. Put your hands under your posterior for support and keeping the legs straight, raise them slowly towards the ceiling to about a 45 degree angle. Hold for a second at the top, then slowly lower them back down. This is an excellent movement to utilize an isometric hold – simply hold your legs at the top 45 degree angle and leave them there for 30 to 60 seconds while continuing to breathe. Everyone wants firmer lower-abs, and this isometric hold will work them like no other. Do it for thirty seconds at the end of each set of leg raises, if you don't mind feeling a little sore the next day.

Day 4: Rest

Repeat Cycle

Advanced Fitness Program

Day 1

5 minute warm-up: Jump Rope

Pistol Squats (25 total reps each side, split into 5-10 sets)
The pistol squat is a one-legged version of the conventional squat. It is amongst the most challenging bodyweight exercises and should not be attempted until the legs have strengthened to the point at which you can perform 50 consecutive parallel squats. It is performed by holding one leg straight ahead parallel to the ground and squatting down and back up with the other leg. Even if your leg strength is well developed, balancing is difficult. Hold your hands out in front of you to help balance. Care must be taken to sit back far enough on the lowering portion of the movement so that the knee does not move forward past the toes. Keep the shin vertical and back as straight as possible, but it will be natural to bend forward somewhat to maintain balance. It may help at first to perform a "box-squat" version of this movement at first – simply sit back on a chair, keep your shin as vertical as possible, and stand up using only one leg to push yourself back to standing. Good luck.

Pull-Ups (30 total reps, split into 3-5 sets)

Grab on to the bar with the hands about shoulder width apart (taking too wide a grip may put some unnecessary strain on your shoulders). Slowly pull yourself up until your chin passes the bar and your chest comes close to being in contact with the bar. The movement should be smooth and strict without any kicking of the legs or wiggling of the lower body to generate momentum. Hold yourself at the top for a second and then lower yourself back down under control.

Unilateral Push-ups (25 total reps each side, split into 5-10 sets)

These one-armed push-ups are a very advanced move and shouldn't even be considered unless you can perform at least 40 consecutive conventional push-ups. They are similar to the regular push-up, except that it will be necessary to take a much wider position with the feet in order to maintain balance – about 6-12 inches wider than shoulder width. Even then, the core stabilization required for the unilateral push-up is extremely strenuous, making it a great workout for the midsection. Be careful when attempting this and take care to monitor any elbow or shoulder joint soreness, treating it with adequate rest.

Side Bend Stretch

Forward Bend Stretch

Diamond Stretch

Day 2: Rest

Day 3

5 minute warm-up: Jump Rope

Interval Sprints – sprint 10 seconds, walk 1 minute

Crunches (50 total reps, split into 2-5 sets)

Leg Raises (25 total reps, split into 3-5 sets)

Ab Wheel Rollouts (25 total reps, split into 2-5 sets) This exercise is optional, but the Ab Wheel is a fantastic tool and a major challenge for the core muscles. It is available for about $10 at Walmart. Simply follow the instructions included in the box and it will increase your core strength in a very short period of time.

Day 4: Rest

Repeat Cycle

Tracking Your Workouts

Keeping a workout journal will be helpful in a number of ways. Besides helping you track your progress to give an accurate depiction of how you're closing in on goals of a particular body weight or measurement, it will help to determine the efficacy of particular exercises. If you've been doing sets of squats for a few months and notice your legs appear more toned and defined, then you know you're on the right track. However, if your shoulders have not made any progress after several months of doing lateral raises, it may be time to switch that exercise for a type of overhead press.

Tracking your results will also assist in establishing the course future workouts should take. For instance, if you were able to perform a maximum of 15 push-ups on Monday, but on Friday, your performance maximum on push-ups declined to 12, then a few days of extra rest is likely required. The opposite is also true, if you have good recovery ability and are making fast progress, you could experiment with exercising with a bit more frequency.

The results in your journal will tell you exactly what is working and what isn't. Review it before and after every workout to move steadily in the direction of your goals.

Little Dogs Setting Good Examples:

Maybe you've had the pleasure of meeting my Grandpuppies, Mickey and Dot. They are "middle-aged" little dogs, but remain as quick and agile as puppies because of their dedication to daily exercise.

When they were very young, Dot and Mickey were taken to a tennis court to exercise about four or five times per week. As a warm up, they would be walked around the perimeter of the tennis court several times. Then, the majority of Mickey's exercise came from chasing his tennis ball. Dot's workout consisted mostly of chasing Mickey down and then screaming at him (for reasons known only to her).

Now, several years later, when taken to a tennis court today, Dot will briskly walk around the perimeter regardless of whether or not there is anyone by her side (though she occasionally stops to sniff things). If Mickey cannot find a person to throw his ball, he will place it on one of the plastic chairs found next to the net and ram the bottom of the chair with his head until it rolls away, giving him something to chase (please if you are going to follow one of their fitness protocols, choose Dot's, not Mickey's).

Dot exercises so she has more energy to stay up late and be a party hostess for visitors. Mickey exercises so he will be more effective in picking fights with the biggest, meanest dogs he sees, despite them usually being about five times his size.

No matter what your fitness goals are, a simple program that utilizes steady progression will help you get there. Ignore the trends and fads, and ignore the overly complicated and often incorrect advice that internet message boards are teeming with. There is no magic routine, only working hard and working smart. Choose a few exercises that you enjoy and stick with them as your core program. Exercise is an essential part of Mickey and Dot's lives. Make it an essential part of yours.

Smart Eating

Healthy/Good Recipes From Good/Healthy People

This chapter will not be a discourse on the evils of certain foods, nor will it be another reworking of a low-carb diet. Take a common sense approach to eating, and if you require further clarification, there are many credible sources available that go into great detail about diet and nutrition.

Instead, what you will find in the following pages is a list of our favorite twenty healthy foods. Include them as components of a smart nutritional plan, and they will serve you well. Bring the list to the grocery store and stock up on some or all of the items on it. Then attach it to the front of your refrigerator, viewing it whenever you are tempted to reach inside for a snack. If you select a snack of blueberries, you'll fill up with healthful anti-oxidants and be less likely to opt for late-night pretzels or chips.

Following that will be several pages of healthy recipes from some of our favorite people – familiar faces at Tranquil Seas Retreats.

20 Priority Foods

Oatmeal

Flax Seed

Blueberries

Tomatoes

Brown Rice

Salmon

Olive Oil

Almonds

Garlic

Avocado

Green Tea

Eggs

Kefir

Bananas

Tuna

Coffee

Spinach

Asparagus

Pomegranate

Dark Chocolate

Breakfast on the Run

<u>Ingredients</u>

1 & 1/3 cups sliced ripe bananas

1 cup skim milk

½ cup plain low fat yogurt

¼ cup wheat germ

2 teaspoons vanilla

1 teaspoon honey

<u>Method</u>

Slice bananas and freeze overnight

Place ingredients in a blender and blend until smooth

Garnish with nutmeg

Bill's Black Bean Soup

Ingredients

1 pound dried black beans

2 quarts water

2 tablespoons olive oil

2 cups chopped onions

1 cup chopped green pepper

2 teaspoons minced garlic

1 teaspoon ground cumin

1 teaspoon oregano

¼ teaspoon dry mustard

1 tablespoon lemon juice

Method

Soak beans in water overnight. After soaking beans, bring to a boil, cover and simmer on low heat for about 2 hours. Heat oil, add onions, and sauté about 5 minutes. Add green pepper and sauté until onions are tender. Stir in remaining ingredients. Add about ¾ cup hot bean liquid, cover and simmer 10 minutes. Add onion seasoning mixture to beans and continue to cook for 1 hour, stirring occasionally. Serve over cooked brown rice and top with chopped green onions

Barb's Chicken Noodle Soup

Ingredients

4 lbs. chicken

1 carrot, shredded

2 medium onions, chopped

2 stalks celery, chopped

1 16 oz. can whole tomatoes, crushed

Salt & pepper to taste

2 bay leaves

½ tsp. Italian seasonings

Thin noodles or rice

Method

Clean chicken well, cut into 1 inch cubes.

Put in pan and cover with water.

Cook until it boils and remove froth.

Add all ingredients except noodles or rice.

Cook 1 hour – remove chicken and let cool.

Break chicken up into small pieces and add to soup.

Bring soup to a boil and add noodles or rice.

Cook noodle 7 minutes. If rice was used, cook rice for 20 minutes.

Let sit 10 minutes.

David Sr's Black-Eyed Pea Dip

Ingredients

3 cups cooked, dry black-eyed peas

½ cup chopped onion

½ cup chopped green pepper

½ cup tomato sauce

¼ cup vinegar

2 tablespoons olive oil

1 tablespoon Worcestershire sauce

¼ teaspoon pepper

¼ teaspoon garlic powder

Method

Place all ingredients in blender or food processor.

Blend for 2 to 3 seconds.

Pieces of pea should be present.

Greg's Stir Fried Beef and Broccoli

Ingredients

¾ pounds round or flank steak

2 teaspoons cornstarch

2 tablespoons soy sauce

3 cups broccoli, peeled, cut into strips

3 cups water

2 tablespoons olive oil

1 cup wedge-cut onion

1 tablespoon minced ginger

2 tablespoons water

Method

Trim fat from steak, slice across the grain in thin slices 1 inch by ¼ inch

Sprinkle with cornstarch and soy sauce. Mix and set aside.

Bring water to a boil, add broccoli, stir, return to boil and cook 2 minutes. Drain immediately and set aside.

Heat oil in wok or large pan until very hot. Add onion and ginger root.

Stir-fry about 30 seconds.

Add steak and stir fry about 2 minutes

Add broccoli and water.

Stir about 1 minute

Serve with rice

Nora's Vegetable Lasagna

Ingredients

6 lasagna noodles (approximately 4 ounces) / 2 quarts water
2 tablespoons olive oil
1 cup chopped onion / 2 teaspoons minced garlic / 1½ cups carrot slices
1¾ cups spaghetti sauce / ½ cup water
1 teaspoon basil / ½ teaspoon oregano
2 eggs / 2 cups low fat cottage cheese / 4 tablespoons parmesan cheese
1 10 ounce package frozen chopped spinach
1 cup quartered and sliced zucchini / 1 cup sliced mushrooms
1 cup shredded part-skim mozzarella cheese / ¼ cup sliced black olives

Method

Cook lasagna noodles in boiling water according to directions on package. Drain, rinse and cover with cold water. Heat olive oil in sauce pan. Add onions, carrots, and garlic. Saute about 10 minutes until tender. Add spaghetti sauce, water and spices. Bring to a simmer. Beat eggs in a separate bowl and blend in cottage cheese, parmesan cheese and vegetables. Spread a thin layer of sauce over bottom of 9x13 baking pan. Cover with layer of noodles, spoon half of cheese mixture over top. Cover with half of sauce. Repeat. Cover with foil and bake at 350F oven for 35 minutes. Remove foil. Arrange olive slices over top and sprinkle with cheese. Bake uncovered about 15 minutes or until center is bubbly. Let cool about 10 minutes to set layers before cutting.

Danielle's Asian Chicken

Ingredients

Boneless chicken tenderloins

Mirin

Soy sauce

Sesame seed oil

Garlic powder

Dried orange peel

Dried onion bits

Dried Thyme

Black pepper

Olive oil for frying/baking

Method

Mix together about a ¼ cup mirin, a few table spoons of soy sauce and a splash of sesame seed oil.

Generously add seasonings to taste.

Place a small amount of olive oil in frying pan or baking pan.

Place chicken in sauce mixture to marinate.

Place chicken and sauce in pan and cook on 350 degrees in oven or medium heat on stove top.

Lee's Stove Top Yams and Apples

Ingredients

1 & ½ pound yams

1 cup water

2 tablespoons SmartBalance spread

3 apples

Sprinkle of cinnamon to taste

Salt to taste

Method

Peel and cut yams in ¼ inch slices.

Place in large skillet.

Pour water over potatoes.

Dot with SmartBalance.

Sprinkle with salt if desired.

Cover, bring to a boil and cook over medium heat for 20 minutes.

Wash, core and slice apples. Spread over potatoes, sprinkle with cinnamon; cover and cook 10 more minutes.

Remove cover and cook until sauce is absorbed about 5 minutes.

Joan's Vegetable Stew

Ingredients

1 Tbsp extra virgin olive oil

1 medium yellow onion - thinly sliced

1 3" or 4" cinnamon stick

1 1/2 tsp ground cumin

2 cups peeled and medium diced (1/2 in cubes) sweet potatoes

1 14 - 16 oz can chick peas drained and rinsed

1 14 1/2 oz can diced tomatoes (juice and all)

1/2 cup pitted green olives (Greek or Italian)

6 Tbsp orange juice

1 1/2 tsp honey

1 cup water

2 cups lightly packed very coarsely chopped Kale leaves

Method

Fry onion in oil in 5-6 qt dutch oven over medium heat until lightly browned. Add cinnamon stick, cumin and cook about 1 minute. Add the sweet potatoes, chickpeas, tomatoes and their juices, olives, orange juice, honey and 1 cup water. Bring to a boil, reduce to medium low and simmer with the lid on. Stir occasionally until the sweet potatoes are barely tender. Stir in kale, cover and cook until wilted. Salt and pepper to taste. Serve with chicken and garlic flavored rice pilaf or couscous.

Karen's Fruit Trifle

<u>Ingredients</u>

Angel Food Cake (store bought is fine)

Yogurt, flavor of your choice

Sugar free instant pudding (or pre made from refrigerator section)

Fresh fruit of your choice (usually use strawberries, kiwi, banana, blueberries)

Cool Whip or whipped cream

<u>Method</u>

In a large bowl, take 1/2 of the angel food cake and break into pieces and place in bowl.

Cover cake with a layer of yogurt and pudding. Cover that with 1/2 the assorted fruit. Sometimes I place some fruit around the sides of bowl for eye appeal. Repeat process with the other half of cake and fruit. Top off with some Cool Whip or whipped cream.

Garnish with a little more fruit if you wish.

Refrigerate until ready to serve!

I have adapted this recipe from a much more calorie and fat dense recipe that used pound cake and heavy custard. This recipe tastes just as good with much less fat and fewer calories!

Barb Snow's Zucchini Bread

Ingredients

3 eggs

2 cups sugar

1 cup vegetable oil

2 cups peeled, raw zucchini, grated

2 teaspoons vanilla extract

3 cups flour

1 teaspoon salt

1 teaspoon baking soda

¼ teaspoon baking powder

3 teaspoons cinnamon

1 cup chopped walnuts (optional)

Method

Beat eggs until light and foamy.

Add sugar, oil, zucchini and vanilla. Mix well.

Combine flour, salt, baking soda, baking powder and cinnamon. Add to zucchini mixture. Stir until well blended. Add nuts.

Pour into two 9x5x3" greased and floured loaf pans. Bake at 350 degrees for 1 hour.

Homeopathy

Stress Damage Control

Recently my Homeopathic practitioner prescribed a remedy for mild reflux. Interesting that after eight years of H2 and proton pump inhibitors from allopathic physicians, it was the homeopathic remedy that actually worked! In a few short weeks the symptoms of reflex were controlled. This reminds me of something I read on the internet:

Brief history of medicine
2000 BC: "Here, eat this root."
1000 BC: "That root is heathen. Here, say this prayer."
1850 AD: "That prayer is superstition. Here, drink this potion."
1940 AD: "That potion is snake oil. Here, swallow this pill."
1985 AD: "That pill is ineffective. Here take this antibiotic."
2012 AD: "That antibiotic doesn't work anymore. Here, eat this root."
-Anonymous

Again, the lesson is to simplify. Moderation is the path.

The history and philosophy of homeopathy continues to fascinate me. An early assertion that like cures was made by Hippocrates about 400 BC, when he prescribed mandrake root, which produced mania, to treat mania, by prescribing a dose smaller than what would produce mania. In the 16th century the pioneer of pharmacology Paracelsus declared that small doses of "what makes a man ill also cures him." but it was Samuel Hahnemann who gave it a name and laid out its principles in the late 18th century. Hahnemann conceived of homeopathy while translating a medical treatise by Scottish physician and chemist William Cullen into German. Being skeptical of Cullen's theory concerning cinchona's action in intermittent fever, Hahnemann ingested some of the bark specifically to see if it cured fever "by virtue of its effect of strengthening the stomach". Upon ingesting the bark, he noticed few stomach symptoms, but did experience fever, shivering and joint pain, symptoms similar to some of the early symptoms of intermittent fever, the disease that the bark was ordinarily used to treat. From this, Hahnemann came to believe that all effective drugs produce symptoms in healthy individuals similar to those of the diseases that they treat. This later became known as the "law of similars" – the most important concept of homeopathy. A few miles from my home there is a hospital named for Samuel Hannemann in Philadelphia, Pennsylvania.

✍Illustrative Journal: by Maria Bohle, Homeopathic Practitioner
Homeopathic Medicine does not treat disease or pathology, homeopathic medicine treats patients who are ill or uncomfortable with the intention of stimulating their immune

system and to bring the 'disease' to the attention of the body so the body can eliminate the disorder. Our bodies produce symptoms in an attempt to keep in balance. If we get sick, the body tries to manage the illness by creating symptoms. If we get a flu, our temperature goes up to kill the bacteria, we get a runny nose to try to flush out the critters, and our bodies attempt to eliminate the illness. Symptoms of a disease or disorder are friends to a homeopath. These symptoms tell us what is wrong with the body. If we can collect those symptoms we can find a remedy to match those symptoms, and with the appropriately small remedy (energy medicine), those symptoms will disappear. Modern medicine is directing energy at the disease state to stop the symptoms, which causes the body to work even harder to re-establish those symptoms. Homeopathic medicine gives the body the symptoms the body feels it needs, which causes the body to end the symptoms, as they are no longer needed.

Our bodies are a wonderfully tuned, precise instrument meant to get us through life "...so that our indwelling, rational spirit can freely avail itself of this living, healthy instrument for the higher purposes of our existence" (Samuel Hahnemann, Aphorism 9 from the Organon of the Medical Arts).

We have learned many ways to help us cope with problems, we can balance our chakras, we can energize our body, we can flush, sooth and nourish with herbal medicines, but there are times when we need a bit more. Diseases, just like the weeds in your garden can be pretty deeply entrenched; actually the roots can go back many, many generations. This is why, as we age, we can often suffer from many of the chronic diseases our parents or grandparents had. Homeopathic medicine can help unlock and free us from these disorders.

Chronic disease can also be like our children – they can have a mind of their own. We may know that we have stomach problems from being upset, or headaches from stress, but unless we can identify the triggers and/or root out the inherited or acquired weakness, those problems will keep re-occurring. Homeopathic medicine matches the disease symptoms of the patient. This fools your body into thinking your symptoms are much, much worse than they are. Treatment with 'similars' both brings the problems to the attention of your body and can cause your body to strengthen against those symptoms, thus eliminating both the problem that caused them and the symptoms that you are experiencing.

When you visit a homeopath, expect a comprehensive interview. Your homeopath must get to know you, your pains and problems, likes and dislikes, trials and tribulations. Homeopaths look for one remedy to help bring your body and mind into balance, and that one remedy also must match the symptoms of the disease you are experiencing. Homeopaths also have great remedies for everyday problems like flu, stomach distress, pink eye and glaucoma or other eye problems, high cholesterol, falls, bruises and strains, vaccination alternatives, etc.

To find a professional homeopath in your area refer to the C.H.C. (Council for Homeopathic Certification) or N.A.S.H. (The North American Society of Homeopaths). Homeopathic Medicine is a serious profession. To ensure that your homeopathic practitioner is properly trained and qualified, s/he should be certified by a professional homeopathic organization. Also, be sure to find someone you feel comfortable with, because you must speak freely to your homeopath. Homeopaths are covered by the HIPA laws. You can be sure a professional will always keep your information private.

Maria T. Bohle, DHM, CHC, RS Hom (NA) is a professional homeopathic practitioner. For more information on Maria, visit the British Institute of Homeopathy's website: www.BihInt.com

Free Radicals

Exactly what are free radicals and why should we want to know about them? They are very hungry. Like little vampires, they want to eat electrons. That is because they have a single unpaired electron and so they go hunting. As they hunt and grab electrons they do damage, really big damage that causes aging. That is why we need to understand these little vampires that bump into our DNA, and take action against their destruction. Before I was born no one had ever heard of these little guys. Now we are taught to take action in the form of ingesting anti-oxidants which are molecules that mix with free radicals and terminate the chain reactions that set off to do damage. So, whether you take Vitamins E, C, beta carotene, or eat nuts, liver, spinach, seeds and fish oils, please do take note of our teaching in this chapter, and the entire book for that matter, calling attention to the changes that need to happen to preclude free radical damage.

Free radicals are formed by white blood cells in the body in order to kill invading bacteria. The free radicals which are formed to kill bacteria, however, also cause damage to DNA and to the walls of normal cells. Since free radicals cause breaks in strands of DNA of normal cells, over time these breaks may contribute to the formation of malignant cells; cancer cells have damaged DNA.

Several different types of free radicals are formed during inflammation, which occurs continuously in the body at low levels and at high levels during a bacterial infection. The process of forming free radicals begins when the neutrophil, more commonly known as the white cell takes oxygen from the air (O2, which has two oxygen molecules) and forms "singlet" (O) oxygen which is composed of a single oxygen molecule).

"Singlet" oxygen is a powerful free radical. The "singlet" oxygen is combines with water (H2O) to form hydrogen peroxide, another type of free radical. This is the same chemical we buy at the drug store in a brown bottle. The peroxide is then broken down and combined with chloride atoms to form HOCl (bleach). This third, very powerful free radical is the major chemical the body uses to kill bacteria. Unfortunately, these compounds the body makes to kill invaders also kill normal cells.

During the process of killing bacteria, the peroxide and bleach also kill the white blood cell that formed the bacteria and many other normal cells in the vicinity of the reaction. The fluid that is formed from dead normal cells and dead bacteria is called "pus". You have probably seen this fluid which is slightly green due to the bleach which is present (you will recall that household bleach has a slight green color). Hydrogen peroxide is not a particularly powerful killer of bacteria but bleach will destroy the DNA of almost any living thing including, normal cells, bacteria or viruses.

The problem is that the free radicals formed in this process ("singlet" oxygen, hydrogen peroxide and bleach), as mentioned, also cause breaks in DNA in normal human cells which may result in formation of malignant cells and are also prominent in the formation of atherosclerosis. Low density lipoproteins deposited in the wall of arteries become oxidized by free radicals and become toxic to surrounding cells in the wall of the artery. This leads to atherosclerosis.

In order to counter the damaging effects of these processes, we should increase our intake of antioxidants to slow the process of atherosclerosis and to avoid damage to DNA of normal cells. The antioxidants will not inhibit the normal response to an infection.

Reference: Prospects for the use of antioxidant therapies. (Review). Drugs 49(3):345-61, 1995 Mar

✎ Illustrative Journal: by Jeannie Francis, Master Herbalist

Among my many travels in life, what I have enjoyed the most is meeting people and learning from them about their many gifts and talents. In my travels, I had the pleasure to meet a group of ladies named the Infinity Reiki Masters. They attended many of the same workshops, programs, and events I had been attending. We became very familiar with each other, shared emails, information and enjoyed seeing each other at these events. We all seemed to connect and enjoy each other's company.

When I had an open house at my reflexology office, I sent out many invitations, through many internet media sites, and mailers. To my surprise, Nora and the "Girls", Infinity Reiki Masters, came out to my event. I was thrilled to have them join in and enjoy celebrating the day with us. Later that day Nora extended to me an invitation to attend one of Tranquil Sea's Retreats to the Pocono Mountains. I was excited about the invitation and just knew I had to go.

On a fine June weekend I traveled to the Blue Mountains of Pennsylvania to attend this wonderful weekend retreat. My intention while attending was for my own self growth. I, like many other people, have bookshelves filled with the best self-help books. I'm well-seasoned in meditation, but I felt I was missing some pieces (peace) of the "puzzle". It was time for me to be willing to take a chance, step out of my comfort zone, adapt to change, and explore new experiences. I am always searching for better understanding of myself, for myself, about my soul and reconnecting with my "quiet".

After arriving at Kirkridge in the Pocono Mountains we were welcomed by Nora and Dave, they helped us locate our rooms, and unpack. Then it was off to the main program room to see what the weekend would hold for me. The opening ceremony was a lot of fun. My mind was boggled by all the wonderful workshops offered and how was I going to fit them all in.

With some time and thought, I managed to figure them all out and then make up my schedule. I was delighted with the workshops that were presented. They were enlightening, educational, and mind-awakening. Along with the workshops, there were many other offerings too, Reiki, Reflexology, massage, foot detox, Tai Chi to greet the day, and more.

On Saturday the group went to Columcille Megalith Park. What a magical place. We were lucky enough to be there on the summer solstice. The park was lively with "children of heart," of all ages. The group got to enjoy the craft show, the music and the vibration of a thousand years in stone. What a pleasure it was to be with a group of women that enjoy the vibrations of nature. I knew in my heart I had found "kindred spirits."

Nora honored me by asking me to give a "wild plant walk" on Sunday morning along the Appalachian Trail. I rejoiced at such a wonderful opportunity to do so. I also prayed I didn't bore anyone with my endless plant trivia. On a sunny warm morning after a great breakfast, I headed out with about forty ladies in tow.

We met many woodland gifts along the way – "weeds" as most of you might call them. However, I introduced the group to Colonial Medicine, plant folk lore and Appalachian plant medicines, along with information on modern day herbal medicine. The group was eager to learn and enjoyed gathering up information about local "weeds."

Following the first retreat, I have since had more chances to teach something that I loved to the others at subsequent retreats. It has been my delight to present educational and fun things with this group of ladies. I had the pleasure of being able to give an herbal tea workshop. We explored blending of many herbs to make the healing teas and tasty mixed beverages to make with herbs. Each person made their own herbal tea mix to take home. It was a delight to see what each person choose to make her own "signature" tea.

In the evenings after supper, evening workshops and yoga, we have time to gather and share. We have always done card readings, palm readings, evenings of "glorious snacking," a wonderful bonding takes place for each one of us, to one another, which is so needed in today's busy world. Most modern women's lives are busy and rushed…to finally have a moment in time, where you're well fed, well heard and in a heart-felt comfy place, we as women can finally take a deep easy breath and come to a calm. In this place of calm, I have found my "quiet."

Herbal Information….June Weeds with helpful properties:

Chickweed is a little known herb which has a wide variety of medicinal and wellness uses. It is an edible plant which can be used as a table vegetable and also to create teas, or "green drinks." It is quite high in Vitamin C, calcium, magnesium and potassium as well. Chickweed is a contact healing herb that relieves pain in addition to stimulating healing as soon as it's applied. It can be used for both internal and external healing. It is also an excellent addition to ointments, poultices and salves. It not only decreases pain, but also helps to reduce swelling such as with torn ligaments. It is especially useful for this when mixed with pure Aloe Vera juice which helps penetrate all three layers of the skin. This in turn allows the chickweed to reach the underlying damaged areas and begin removing the pain and starting the healing process. Chickweed in tea form is excellent for use as an acne wash, and it can even be added to a bath to help with sores, rashes, boils and burns.

Plantain is edible. Harvest the young, tender leaves for use in a salad, or steamed and used as a spinach substitute. The leaves do get tough quickly, so make sure to harvest only the youngest leaves. The immature flower stalks may be eaten raw or cooked. If you're really adventuresome, you can harvest the seeds. They are said to have a nutty flavor and may be parched and added to a variety of foods or ground into flour. The leaves, seeds and roots can all be made into an herbal tea.

Comforting ways to invigorate the body:

Facial Wash

Keeping a healthy PH for the skin is very important. This facial wash or spray is great for the skin anytime:

1 cup white vinegar
1 tea bag of Eyebright
1 tea bag hawthorn
1 teabag of peppermint
1 teaspoon Rosemary
1 teaspoon of Arnica
1 vitamin C tablet (chewable) crushed

Heat vinegar to 100 degrees; add all the above ingredients and let steep 24 hrs. Strain and place in a spray bottle and keep in your bathroom. Mist your face at night and in the morning.

Foot Soak

1 cup Epsom salts
½ cup of Dead Sea salt
½ cup Mint leaves
6 drops tea tree
3 drops of Lemon oil
1 cup vinegar

Mix all dry ingredients and store in a clean glass jar. To prepare bath take out ¼ cup dry mix and add to 1 cup heated vinegar to a large foot pan with hot water. Soak your feet and add more hot water when it cools down. This mix will help relax tired feet, detox feet and bring about better health and balance to the body.

Jeannie Francis can be contacted through her website at www.spirittosoleconnection.com

Loss and Healing

Handling Life's Most Upsetting Events

Coping with loss and grief can be one of the most difficult times in a person's life. It certainly was for me when my father died when I was a small child. It was also difficult to move from the east coast to the west coast leaving my friends and family behind.

Grief manifests from many different kinds of loss. The person experiencing the loss often has a unique response to it.

There is loss when a parent dies or a business associate or a friend. There is loss and grief too when a significant other/spouse exits the relationship abruptly. We can be shocked by a loss when a friend dies from a mugger's gunshot, or sudden heart attack or auto accident. I had often wondered at a personal level if it was easier to cope with loss after caring for a terminally ill person and having time to process the grief during the illness, or in the case of a fast heart attack that takes us by shock.

The end of a long term relationship can feel like a death due to the level of attachment. The inability to process grief is exasperated by triggers of holiday events, places and things of commonality without the loved one.

The inability to skillfully process the grief can create a major clinical depression complete with anger toward a higher power, the deceased, the doctors who failed and even others who try to help. There can be sleep and eating disturbances, anxiety and even survivors guilt. Without a process, program support system or counseling, it can take longer to truly heal.

The purpose of the cultural ceremonies used for generations is to help mitigate the effects of the grief and loss process. The advantage of working with a professional grief counselor is enormous. During one of our retreats I invited a nationally recognized grief counselor to be our keynote speaker.

Toni organized and ran the first pet loss bereavement program in NJ. Her description of the process of grief during the first three months after loss was outstanding and informative in a way that amazed me. One fascinating observation was that every single retreat participant attended that lecture. At first they felt it might be a workshop only for those who had recent loss, but as they sat and learned from this extraordinary woman they soon realized her teachings were applicable to all present.

Illustrative Journal: by Toni Griffith, Grief Counselor
At a recent Tranquil Seas Retreat, we explored the nature of loss in relation to the ability to cope with the wide range of emotional

upheaval that usually comes with the many losses we face in our lifetimes starting in childhood and on throughout our adult lives.

What is loss?

Loss is the disappearance of something or someone that we value or valued in our past, present or future.

Loss is never simple. It is almost always stressful and more complicated than it first appears to be. It is a common loss to lose the car keys or your wallet. The results are not always tragic and complicated. But sometimes they can cause us to unravel based on when it happens and how long it takes to straighten things out. We have to deal with many losses in the course of our life. Moving to a different house or school. Loss of friends, loss of jobs, loss of health, loss of relationships. Death is perhaps one of the strongest and deepest losses.

Grief is the reaction to loss.

That reaction occurs on several levels: Emotional, physical, behavioral, cognitive and spiritual. Grief is a process and it takes as long as the person experiencing it needs to get through the process. It cannot be hurried, but it can stall.

Many losses occur in childhood and can carry through to adulthood. Loss of a parent or parent figure is particularly difficult because it continues on with us as we graduate high school, attend our proms, receive awards, get jobs, get married…all without that person being physically present. It occurs in the past but carries on into the future.

Ken Doka wrote the book *Disenfranchised Grief* in 1989, explaining the concept and giving it the name that we use today. Some losses are unrecognized by society and are called disenfranchised. Pet loss is one. Death of an ex-spouse, death of a good friend at work, stigmatized deaths such as homicides and suicides all are generally not considered by others to be the strong stressors that they are.

There are many grief processes that have been written about in the past several years. William Worden gives the process a task orientation. They include:

Acknowledging the loss.

Notice that the word is AKNOWLEDGE, not accept. Acceptance is something that takes much longer and sometimes does not happen.

Feel the emotions…meaning also the pain.

This is especially difficult when as a society we are used to doing and having many things at our disposal to lessen pain. Alcohol, drugs, retail therapy, avoidance are all ways that we use to not feel the pain of grief. This usually prolongs the process.

Adjust to the environment without the person. We have to establish new routines, do holidays differently, re-do life in way that works without the person.

Reinvest the energy of grieving into reliving life. When we take the energy of grief and are able to put it to use in different or new ways such as a new job, new relationships, travel, education and we are able to start living with a new appreciation for life.

Thomas Attig has given us a soul process called "brokenness". He looks at what is broken and what remains unbroken in the grief process. He looks at the spirit and the soul and what is mendable and what may bend but does not break. It helps us to understand that the bonds forged in life continue even after death.

At the retreat I was aware that many of the people there were in various phases of grief work. They were grieving for friends who had recently died, mothers and husbands, as well as near death experiences. All are life changing. There were emotions that were almost visible. Wounds that would still require time and lots of emotional effort to heal. There was a case of disenfranchised grief from a nuclear engineer who was grieving the Japanese counterparts who were dangerously staying at a nuclear reactor damaged by an earthquake following a tsunami. No one recognized her dismay and distress for these "heroes" who were at extreme risk of dying of radiation poisoning. There was anger when old losses were recalled. Life is not always kind and loss is almost never forgotten. Forgiveness was a subject presented but with the concern that forgiveness as well as acceptance come later in the process. But, often without these two the grief process itself can remain unresolved.

Grief work is a physical, emotional, behavioral, and spiritual process that changes our inner being. Cognitive understanding helps us navigate the unchartered waters that enable us to enter the sea of tranquility that we search for in our quest for a more positive life.

Toni Griffith, LCSW, BCD

Loss of Those Closest

The loss of a husband/wife/partner is felt in every area of our being. The pain permeates our core and we progress through many stages to recover and ultimately accept the loss. The spouse is someone we share our lives with in a way unique to that institution of marriage/civil union. Day in and day out the ups and downs and in the good times and bad, we blend in a union of intimate togetherness. When death occurs the survivor experiences a unique suspension in time as they heal and recover from the sudden end to life as they knew it. In the illustrative journal that follows, Maria details the loss of a husband after four decades together.

✑Illustrative Journal: by M. T.

Laughter and friendships were so far away, life had lost a lot of its meaning in the wake of my husband's passing, 38 years was a lifetime, and I was numb. Days passed and I was on autopilot, one foot in front of the other without any divisions of free time, family time or fun time. The Tranquil Seas Retreat was holding a "grief session," I could certainly use any help I could get at this point in my life. Little did I know that this experience would be the gateway into a new and rewarding experience.

I had a delightful and wondrous weekend, my fellow attendees were warm, real and diversified in their talents and life experiences. I met some super new friends, many I suspect who will enrich my life with their companionship for years to come. The featured speakers were all excellent and experts in their fields. Caring people who took the time to offer their knowledge to bring us up to a greater awareness of both ourselves and the blessings our life has to offer.

From feeling my life was over to exploring at a megalithic park, walking a meditation labyrinth, and practicing some healing yoga and Qigong exercises in the morning sunlight – I discovered a whole new life, in a sense I was reborn to many new and wondrous experiences. No, the grief is not gone, but I am learning to take it in stride and enjoy the blessings that surround me. I greatly look forward to the next retreat and to renew friendships I have made and to make new friends.

The Passing of Those Who Gave Us Life

It does not matter the age of our parents when they pass, they are always Mom and Dad. Whether their death is at thirty-five or one-hundred, it is no more or less painful. The adage that "she lived to a ripe old age" really doesn't cut it when you enter a hospital room late at night and see the body of a very old woman who has just passed. If she was your mother there is grief, loss and pain.

The other thing I have learned in this lifetime is that death always comes as a surprise. Irrespective of the length of an illness or however long doctors predicted a loved one had to live, we are always shocked and surprised and expect and want more time with them. We want to ask more questions learn more about who they really were and what they thought... and yes, to tell them one more time that we love them.

Toni Cristinzio explains her grief after the death of her mother and her work in grief counseling in the next illustrative journal.

✎Illustrative Journal: by Toni Cristinzio

The trip to Kirkridge came at a time in my life when I was at a crossroads in many ways. Within the preceding four years, I experienced a series of major life changes, one right after another without much of a break in between. A few of the life changes included moving back to New Jersey in order to live with my mom who was my best friend, to find out that she had stage III/IV gastroesophageal cancer. The cancer later spread to her brain, meaning that in addition to being best friends, I would also become her caregiver and cheerleader, and after her death, assume responsibility for taking care of her estate, deal with changed family dynamics, and clean out and sell my childhood home. Although with the ending of the latest cycle settling of the Estate, I thought I was "free," I later found out that I was still trapped in limbo/funk so to speak...where I needed to honor and let my past go in order to live my *new* life to the fullest.

When I heard about the Kirkridge trip, it sounded interesting, but I was somewhat leery to enter into the world of energy/healing. So I asked spirit if it was in my highest and best to attend. The answer was "yes." The peace and serenity at Kirkridge was just what I needed – to get away from my everyday world.

I enjoyed all the activities we did. In the mornings, I tried to spend some meditative time outside in nature before starting the activities. The comparison of world religions was fascinating. The self-protection class was a lot of fun and informative. Doing yoga again felt natural, although I had lost a lot of flexibility from not doing it for so long. The old adage of "when the student is ready the teacher appears" is very true…and is exactly what happened. The guest speaker at this particular retreat was Toni Griffith, who is a grief/life transition counselor. After speaking with her, I realized that I may not have dealt with all the changes as well as I thought I had. Spirit also gave me signs that she is the one that I'm to work with to help me assimilate/understand all the changes and more forward, which brings me to the most intense part of the trip for me…

Our excursions on the Kirkridge grounds included a labyrinth, a chapel in the woods, and what I call a "mini-Stonehenge." The first day we went there, I think I was probably too in awe of the beauty and energy of the location to really comprehend the energy of the place. The second day, I had a totally different experience and it all started at the chapel in Columcille. This time, when I entered the chapel, I was the only one in it. I decided to sit on the bench directly opposite the door. While soaking in the energy I suddenly started crying. I fought back the tears, since I hate to cry. While observing my surroundings in detail, I noticed that the floor is actually made up of different slabs of concrete with etchings. The slab directly under my feet had three etchings: they appeared to be a dolphin, Stonehenge, and Celtic cross – all important symbols to me that have an extremely strong connection with my mom. Then all of sudden, I felt her around me and could no longer hold back the tears.

In addition, to these signs that I shared with you, I also received many others during my three days in Kirkridge that my guides, masters, teachers, angels, parents and other loved ones were there with me watching over me and my future. So what does my future hold for me? That remains to be seen. However, I need to remember to trust and have faith, and just know that what I need will be provided at the right time.

Healing At Home: Putting Your Emotions Into Words

Journaling is the writing of random thoughts that come and go during the course of day. It helps to journal during the first year after grief and loss become part of one's life. The suggested format is to write in both the morning and the afternoon but not late into the evening. Just write everything that comes into your mind as it relates to the grief process.

Journaling can cut through the confusion and provide clarity and inner strength and is a valuable record of where to begin in therapy. Tranquil Seas has provided several journaling workshops and will in the future continue to teach this valuable tool.

Music

The Many Benefits Of Playing A Musical Instrument

My dad was born in Italy and made his way to America with his parents as a young child. They were processed at Ellis Island, with papers from Naples. By all accounts my dad, Ben, was fascinated by music and gifted with musical ability at an early age. He left high school a few months short of graduating and made his way to California to seek fame and fortune in the music industry. After a few years he returned to New York City with several members of his big band and a brand new cornet. The cornet resembles the trumpet, but has a shorter and narrower shank than a trumpet mouthpiece. The long-model cornet is generally used in concert bands in the United States. His band instrumentation consisted of five saxophones, two altos, two tenors, and one baritone, a cornet, drums, banjo, violin and clarinets. We have photographs of Dad's band playing at several of the classic nightclubs in New York City. In addition to the performance of big band music, my dad wrote lyrics with a poetic genius.

Life and family responsibilities eventually became the priority and Dad shifted over to marriage, raising a family and his work as a chef. He taught me how to read music, play the piano, clarinet and sax before I was eight. I found the clarinet to be my first love and soon found myself in private lessons a few times a week to study the woodwinds. Dad always sat with me in the evenings to listen to what I had learned and monitor my musical progress. By the end of fourth grade the school system made available a band practice and group lessons, so I continued my studies.

It was around this time that my father passed away after a short illness. I continued my study of music because I had a passion for it, but also in his honor. During junior and senior high school I played clarinet in the concert band, marching band and symphony orchestra. One of the top five activities of my life was learning formations for the marching band and playing at those wonderful football games!

Each year the band traveled to the Poconos to train for the marching band season and the lessons learned there about teamwork and the value of community leadership as captain of my squad proved valuable in later life. In retrospect, there is no doubt that those early years set the tone of the Tranquil Seas Retreat locations since much of our work is done in the Poconos.

Deep bows to my dad, Ben D'Ecclesis. Now, we have all heard it skips a generation which did not prove to be accurate in my case. My son was born long after my father passed, but before he even went to kindergarten, Dave asked for piano lessons and learned to read music. He practiced without being reminded and demonstrated the same musical ear and passion for music that I had seen in my father many years before. Music was then and will continue to be a major passion in our family.

Meditation Without Meditating

Few things in this world are more expressively powerful than music – it includes physical, emotional, and spiritual components. The act of creating music helps enhance focus and concentration, teaching how to truly listen. It is an easy way to separate from conscious thought, shutting off the mental chaos of a long workday, being a conduit for inward focus.

A performing musician knows that when onstage, the connection with the audience is a one-of-a-kind encounter, where inward focus and outward connection can be felt at the very same time. In other words, it is a meditative act crossing paths and intertwining with a communal spirit. The experience is breathtaking and indescribable – spirituality, that, by definition, is impossible to define.

The concentration that is necessary to progress to better levels of musicianship is very similar to that of meditation, yet for many, it is easier to attain. After all, many will be better able to bring straying focus back to a chord progression than to breathing. Not only will the ability to truly listen be enhanced, but the ability to "stop listening" will also develop. Many will agree that shutting off the mental faucet is one of the most difficult skills to master. Best of all, playing music is fun; a sentiment that isn't shared by all those who have attempted conventional meditation.

Social Interaction Through Music

Playing a musical instrument gives you a life-long pursuit for which you can set and achieve both short and long-term goals, but rarely arrive at true mastery. It is for this reason that playing music becomes so valuable. With no pre-conceived end point in mind, it provides a tool that develops the ability to live in the moment and enjoy the journey rather than focus solely on the horizon. Not only will it result in a lifetime of near-meditative relaxation, but playing an instrument also opens up many opportunities for social interactions with like-minded people.

Musical ability affords one not only individual freedom to explore creativity in solitude if so desired, but also the connections to a huge community of thoughtful, creative people who share a similar passion. Learning to selflessly contribute to the creative concept of a group is a type of fulfillment that is unique to this particular form of artistic expression. Neither writers, nor painters have the same opportunities that musicians have to experience growth on inter-personal levels. The ensemble dynamic of music can instill the ability to generate selfless contributions within a group of people. This can easily translate to better relationships in other areas of life.

Beginning Guitar

Because of the popularity and portability of the acoustic guitar, a course in guitar basics is offered at Tranquil Seas Retreats to honor the importance of music education and appreciation. The guitar is a commonly used instrument in a great variety of musical styles. From Segovia's classical style, to Joe Pass' solo jazz, to Steve Vai's virtuosity, to Bob Dylan's strumming, the instrument can be both a tool for self-accompaniment, as well as part of an ensemble.

Trends and fads in musical styles have come and gone, but the guitar has remained a respectable element of music. Expect that to continue for many, many years.

A Few Guitar Technique Fundamentals

While there is no substitute for guitar instruction by a qualified teacher, what follows are a few basics that will come in handy if you take our advice about the myriad benefits of playing an instrument and decide to pick up a guitar for the first time.

Experienced players may also find it helpful to review this section to evaluate their technical foundation.

Posture

The guitar may be played seated or standing up. Classical guitarists almost always play sitting down, whereas rock guitarists will usually play while standing. The use of a shoulder strap for the guitar is essential if standing. Your guitar should hang over the shoulder and rest against the abdomen. Too high a placement can make open-position chord playing difficult, but if the guitar is too low, it can strain the left wrist.

When seated, the casual approach is to let the guitar rest on the leg that shares the same side of the dominant hand. An alternative when playing sitting down is the classical method, where the guitar is rested on the left (or non-dominant) leg, and the neck of the guitar is held at an upward (about 45-degree) angle to allow for better placement and freedom of movement of the left and right hands. Whether seated or standing, the posture of the back should be straight.

Left hand technique

When playing the guitar, the function of the left (or non-dominant) hand is to press the strings down in contact with the frets in order to sound the desired notes. The left fingers must be in position before the strings are struck by the right hand. The thumb acts as an anchor which allows the right amount of pressure to come from the fretting fingers. The other fingers should be arched as to allow the tips to come in contact with the guitar's fret-board.

When fretting a string, it should be held down between two frets, slightly behind the target fret. This will cause the string to vibrate between the fretted note and the saddle of the guitar, which results in the desired pitch.

Right hand technique

Right (or dominant) hand technique can involve playing with the fingers or a pick. Most classical, flamenco, and folk guitarists will choose to play with their fingers, and with a few exceptions, most rock, jazz and blues guitarists choose to play with a pick. Picks produce a louder, clearer tone and will often allow for more speed in striking the strings. Finger-style players enjoy more versatility with their right hand technique, an example of which is jazz guitarist Joe Pass' ability to play bass lines, melody lines, and chords simultaneously while playing solo guitar.

When playing, the right forearm should rest lightly along the top of the guitar's body, which leaves it free to move and pluck or strum the strings. The playing area for the right hand is usually between the bottom of the guitar's neck and above the bridge. Proper right hand position can be attained when seated by draping the right arm over the top of the guitar, and the right hand should be held loosely outstretched over the strings between a 60-degree and 90-degree angle.

✒ Illustrative Journal: by Dave, Guitar Guy

Hi, my name's Dave. Attendees of Tranquil Seas Retreats may remember me as the guy who carries their luggage. However, if you were to look beyond my exterior, you would see more than just a bellhop. You'd see a guy who is truly passionate about picking things up, carrying them a pre-determined distance, and then putting them down. Now look even deeper, past the bellhop, past the picking up and putting down. What you'll see is a guy who does a lot of chin-ups to develop the "pulling muscles" of the upper back for strenuous suitcase lifting, and because the act of lifting myself upwards is metaphorically positive. Finally, look beyond the chin-ups and you'll see a passionate musician. A lifelong musician, who began with piano lessons at the age of five and became hooked on the little dots on staff paper which turned into beautiful sounds when channeled through the piano. A few years later, I switched to the eminently more portable electric guitar. It is the one and only interest I can unequivocally state that I will pursue until the day I die.

Let's discuss for a moment the emotional potency of music. If there's a force in the universe that is more powerful than music in influencing emotional response and stirring passion in people, then I don't know what it is. Musicians truly have the ability to transform the emotional state of their audience. There are countless examples of music bringing entire stadiums full of people to crescendos of excitement that would be impossible to experience through other mediums. If your only familiarity with musicianship consists of sitting in a room alone, holding an acoustic guitar tight against your chest and feeling the soothing vibrations of one continually strummed "open E" chord, rest assured that is a worthwhile activity.

Those who have chosen to study an instrument further are well aware that it is an interest that is not only continually rewarding, but also profoundly enlightening. Utilizing amalgamations of different styles, musician's creations can become illustrations of inclusion. For those people that tolerate compartmentalization in society, this is a lesson worth learning. Simply put, you would be much more likely to find people harshly debating Protestantism versus Catholicism than you would find people angrily pitting blues against rock music.

Likewise, musical groups were composed of racially mixed performers long before it become commonplace in the sports community, or pretty much anywhere else for that matter. Case in point, I'm sure we've all seen one of the dozens of documentaries that chronicle Jackie Robinson's career. As I'm sure you're aware, Mr. Robinson made history by being the first African American Major League Baseball player, helping to change America for the better by challenging the notion of segregation. This seminal event occurred when Mr. Robinson made his debut for the Brooklyn Dodgers in 1947. Now look back a decade prior, when African-American guitarist Charlie Christian, arguably the father of the modern guitar solo, joined white bandleader Benny Goodman's orchestra. Mr. Christian, with African-American musicians Teddy Wilson and Lionel Hampton, sat alongside white drummer Gene Krupa to perform with Mr. Goodman at Carnegie Hall in 1938.

If you want to see countless instances of acceptance, look to the world of music. Musicians have often set great examples for us all by blending musical styles and celebrating differences, being inclusive instead of divisive. That's why music has long been on the cutting edge of social progress.

My twenty years of guitar playing experience does more than make me an expert at moving heavy things (nothing is a better workout that dragging guitar amplifiers around every Saturday night). It also allows me to teach guitar performance methods to the wonderful people at Tranquil Seas Retreat.

I'm known on the Philadelphia music scene for my humble attitude (insert rim-shot here), so I'll be the first to suggest that if you only attend one guitar workshop this year, make it the one at Tranquil Seas Retreat. Its content includes the technical elements of playing, such as proper hand position and technique. We also cover melodic embellishments and touch on a bit of music theory. You'll learn how to use your natural creativity for self-expression, build a foundation of the "rules" of guitar playing…then learn how to break those very same rules in the interest of originality.

The focus though is on the lessons that guitar playing can teach us that are applicable to everyday life. Take improvisational skills, for example. The ability to improvise will assist you in many situations. It goes without saying that those who focus on creative solutions will succeed much more often that those who dwell on the circumstances that led up to the problem. Improvisation is a skill that can be practiced, and there is no better place to practice it than on the fret-board of a beautiful guitar.

Performing music has taught me lessons that have translated into every area of life. It's a stalwart bastion of purity in an increasing polluted world. I make music not for the money (obviously), not for the women (maybe not as obvious), not for an excuse to travel, not to satisfy my ego, not for complementary food and drinks, and not for the love of performing. No, I make music because it is coming out of me, and I will continue to do so far beyond the point where there is absolutely no one else listening. You, my friend, should do the same. I suggest that if you already play an instrument, that you devote more time to it. If you don't currently own a guitar, go buy one immediately. Right now.

Seriously, put this book down for an hour, go to the music store and invest $100 dollars in an acoustic guitar. The money you spend on it is one of the only investments that will truly provide a guaranteed return. Bring your guitar to the Tranquil Seas Guitar Workshop and we'll get started.

Here are a few tips that I always share with the workshop's students...

(1) Warm Up and Keep Warm

Whether lifting heavy things or playing an instrument, a good warm up will help you perform better and avoid discomfort. Warm up your fingers by running up and down basic scale shapes, starting very slowly and building up to a moderate speed. This will help you to loosen up as well as preventing cramping in the forearms when playing for longer periods of time.

Not to be overlooked is the importance of keeping the hands physically warm. Playing with shivering fingers is not only unpleasant, but it can greatly hinder performance. I've played countless gigs in freezing winter temperatures that had my hands frozen after dragging guitars, amplifiers and other assorted equipment through snowy city streets.

The best way to thaw hands is to run them under warm water for a few minutes. In the absence of a functional sink (which is disturbingly common at rock clubs), have someone hold a cigarette lighter under your hands while you vigorously rub them together. I've utilized this method frequently in my gigging career, as, at the aforementioned clubs, cigarette lighters outnumber properly functioning sinks at an estimated ratio of 250,000 to 1 (give or take).

Whether you're playing a gig or just strumming a few chords as you sit on your back porch with friends, having warm hands will make playing much easier.

(2) Start with the "Big 7"

Learn commonly used chords first. I suggest the "Open Position" voicings of E, A, D, G, C, Em, Am. The fingerings for these chords can be found in most any guitar method book, or at my blog, sharpenedguitar.com.

Using these, you'll be able to play a huge cross-section of popular music. Many songs you'll hear on the radio – from Bob Dylan, to Green Day, to Rhianna – utilize only three or four chords, so you're much closer than you think to having an arsenal of chords that will enable you to perform your favorite songs.

A method for learning new chords is to look up a new one online or in a chord book, then work your fingers into position. Pluck each applicable note individually and make sure each of them sound clear and clean. If you get a bum note, shift your fingertips around until it becomes strong and distinct.

When your grip on a chord has it sounding perfect, pick up your fingers and extend them straight out like you're flicking water droplets off of your fingertips. Then grab the chord again. Though it may take a while for your mind and fingers to synch up on a newly learned chord shape, practicing this drill will help you develop the ability to grip the shape in fractions of a second.

If you watch performance footage of Elvis, Billy Ray Cyrus, Sheryl Crow, or just about every country singer who has ever used an acoustic guitar as a stage prop, you'll notice that they struggle any time they have to execute a chord change that involves moving more than one of their fingers at the same time. Practicing the essential art of smoothly transitioning between chords will have you performing at higher levels of musicianship than many of the "pros."

(3) Tap Your Foot

Whether standing, sitting, or hanging from the stage rafters like 90's era Eddie Vedder, you should always tap your foot when playing. This will develop your sense of timing and assist your hands in maintaining steady rhythm. The legendary John Lee Hooker made stomping his foot a part of his signature sound. The percussive thud of his boot against the wooden floor of the studio sound-stage with each downbeat was a signature element of John Lee's early recordings, back when his only instrumentation was guitar, voice, and boot.

Learning to tap your foot is essential for developing consistent rhythm, but it should not be underestimated as a form of accompaniment. I remember being quite inspired by a musician performing blues standards on the corner of 6th & South Street in Philadelphia. He had taken a ride cymbal from a drum set and positioned it under his feet as to tap down on it from above on each down beat and tap it from the side on alternating upbeats. He also stomped his boot against the concrete occasionally, to give the illusion of a bass drum. The result very closely resembled that of a full drum-kit. I was so impressed that I tipped him $3, which is, quite frankly, more than I've ever tipped anyone for anything (just kidding, sort of). As evidenced by the street musician in Philadelphia, a simple tool can be turned into an incredibly unique resource.

Practice tapping your foot along with a drum machine or metronome; doing so will forge excellent rhythm. Steady rhythm is a weak point of many guitarists, including professionals. Even the most blazing fret-board technique will be hampered by poor coordination between the hands and cause choppy, inconsistent strumming. Underdeveloped rhythm skills and poor sense of tempo are evident even when playing unaccompanied, and even more obvious when performing alongside a drummer or percussionist.

Having a rock-solid sense of timing and coordinated hands working in unison will distinguish you as a good player, even if you've only mastered a few chords. If the only chords you know are the seven I mentioned earlier, but you develop the ability to smoothly transition between them and pair it with great rhythm and timing, you'll have a great foundation of functional playing ability. Other chords, scales, and various techniques will be easy to add later once you've developed a solid base.

A great exercise is to tap your foot and strum a chord. Tap out eight beats and then strum a different chord. As you get more comfortable and accurate with your chord changes, tap your foot and strum a different chord every four beats. Then every two. Eventually, you'll be able to switch chords each beat in perfect time. Even if that level of skill seems like it's in the very distant future, I promise you, it's well within your ability to learn.

Build your progress on small, consistent steps.

(4) Listen to the Good

John Lee Hooker once said "There's only two kinds of music; good and bad." Listen to and learn from all styles of music, across a broad spectrum of genres. Most people have very diverse and wide-ranging tastes in music. Guitar virtuoso Steve Vai has said that one of his favorite genres to draw inspiration from is Bulgarian wedding music. Likewise, many guitarists have been heavily influenced by Niccolo Paganini, an Italian violinist who lived in the 1800's. If any of this sounds strange, think about this: Would you rather hear a guitar solo that was inspired by one of Paganini's violin runs? Or would you rather hear the umpteenth version of some poseur's imitation of Eddie Van Halen?

Our favorite talented artists, our awful guilty pleasures, our mood music for certain occasions – a typical I-Pod shuffle might play Christina Aguilera right after Miles Davis – that type of diversity comes in very useful when you're learning an instrument. For example, if you play mostly acoustic rock, learning bossa nova rhythms will not only help you become a more well-rounded player, but it will give to a grab-bag to choose from for some fantastic fusions of musical styles. Remember Paul Simon's use of African rhythms on his Graceland album? For me, that added much needed excitement to Simon's boring folk music (If you're a Simon and Garfunkel fan, please, forgive my candor).

Good and bad can be found everywhere – in every genre you'll find both John Coltranes and a Kenny G's. I'll bet even the esteemed Mr. G would tell you you'd be better off listening to Coltrane. Rather than further discussing the most obnoxiously atrocious saxophonist in history, allow me to suggest a few places to begin when searching for new music. Next time you want to expand your horizons, here are just a few of the many icons of "good" music…

First, the non-guitarists:

Niccolo Paganini – A classical violin virtuoso that lived an extreme "rock-n-roll lifestyle" two-hundred years before rock-n-roll was invented. Recordings of his compositions performed by contemporary violinists are widely available.

Miles Davis – The "Godfather of Cool" and creator of an absolutely transcendental jazz album, "Kind of Blue," Miles is required listening for everyone who doesn't live in a cave.

Ravi Shankar – You hippies remember Ravi as the world's foremost Sitar player. This is a good departure point for those looking to explore the music of different cultures.

Jimmy Cliff – Chances are you've heard a few Jimmy Cliff songs and may not even be aware that it was him. Do yourself a favor and listen to a few more.

Tupac Shakur – I know what you're thinking. But I wanted to include a rapper on this list, and Tupac was the only one I know of that ever recorded a song about how much he loves his Mom.

Now, the six-string heroes:

Andres Segovia – Segovia is a legendary classical guitarist who performed into his 80's and lived into his 90's. Playing beautiful songs may or may not be responsible for his longevity, but I suggest we all pick up nylon-stringed guitars and try to find out.

Wes Montgomery – Wes Montgomery took his lack of formal musical training and developed a virtuoso melodic style that still sounds current decades after his death.

Joe Pass – A pioneer in the art of solo jazz guitar, Joe Pass took the instrument to an unaccompanied place usually reserved only for the piano. As a bonus, familiarity with his music will help you settle any debate about who is the all-time-greatest Italian-American jazz musician.

BB King – He may play blues, but it is as uplifting as it is inspirational. Notice his "conversational" style of playing where he uses guitar phrases to mimic questions and answers. He continues to tour well into his 80's, having worked anecdotes about Viagra in his sets.

Jimi Hendrix – Electric guitar innovation at its height, Jimi Hendrix remains the standard by which all others are measured. He supplemented his immense talent by wearing some really crazy looking pants.

(5) You're Only a Half-Step Away

Remember, when you hit a "wrong" note, you're only a half-step away from a "right" one. For example, let's say you're playing in the key of G major, which includes the notes G, A, B, C, D, E, F#. One minute you're playing a great solo, but the singer's big egotistical head sways in front of you and blocks out the stage lighting, causing you to land on C#. When taken in context of a G key signature, C# is a sour note – the dreaded "tri-tone" in fact, an interval that some medieval composers were severely reprimanded for including in compositions. What to do?

Remember, you're only a half-step away from a melodic note in either direction. On a guitar, move one fret up to D or one fret down to C and you're back in key. Instead of hearing it as a "bum note," the audience will think you've built up dramatic tension using dissonance. You can even repeat your "mistake" several times to make it seem like it was done intentionally to be avant-garde.

In the interest of accuracy, let me point out that in music there is no such thing as a mistake. There is only serendipity, chance, and good fortune. If only all of life were so simple and beautiful. Fortunately, a guitar is never far away…

If you're interested in more of Dave's music musings, visit his blog at: http://sharpenedguitar.wordpress.com

Astrology

Path For The Spirit

Much like energy healing and Vedic palmistry, the system of Astrology has ancient origins. Today, it is utilized for a number of different purposes, the most common of which include analysis of personality traits, compatibility between people, behavioral reactions, and the connection between the conscious and subconscious mind. Like palmistry, it can be used to give guidance and provide clarity when life seems unclear.

Based on the notion that the movement of the planets has an impact on components of the Universe which of course include us, analysis of astrology can help us make sense of some of our tendencies that…well, it can help us makes sense of some of our tendencies that don't make any other kind of sense. Accordingly, it can be a valuable tool in introspection and self-discovery, as well as a guide in relationships where contrasting behaviors can become a distraction. Besides that, discussions about astrology can be a lot of fun, especially once you become familiar with the many facets involved.

For those unfamiliar with the moon sign, the ascendant, and the houses, you will find that astrology goes far beyond the "Daily Horoscope" section of the newspaper.

✍Illustrative Journal: by Danielle Stella, Astrologer

The main components of an astrological chart are the sun sign, the moon sign, and the ascendant. Most of us commonly associate astrology with the sun sign only. It refers to the position of the sun at the time of an individual's birth, which influences character, lifestyle and social interaction. However, what many do not realize is the impact of sun signs is altered by the moon sign, ascendant and the alignment of the planets Mercury, Venus, Mars, Jupiter, Saturn, Uranus, Neptune, and Pluto at the time of a person's birth. The moon sign, for example, affects how your outward emotions are perceived.

Complexities extend far beyond what is commonly thought of when the subject of astrology is mentioned. This is essential to comprehend if you get a detailed astrological reading. Basic knowledge of these components will help you to make sense of any analysis you receive on this topic.

While revealing your moon sign is a complex process, you can determine your sun sign by simply finding your birthday in the list below. Characteristics common to the signs are included, as well as the planet, element, mode most distinguishing trait, anatomical relation, and attributes worth cultivating (applicable to your ascendant sign).

Aries: March 21st – April 20th

Planet: Mars

Element: Fire

Mode: Cardinal (self-starter)

Human Anatomy Association: Head/Brain

Characteristics: Individuality… Action oriented… Impulsive… Direct… Hasty… Love of new challenges

Cultivate: Moderation… Patience

Taurus: April 21st – May 20th

Planet: Venus

Element: Earth

Mode: Fixed (immovable)

Human Anatomy Association: Neck/Throat

Characteristics: Appreciation of beauty… Love of music… Stubborn… Dislikes change… Good with children

Cultivate: Adaptability… Foresight

Gemini: May 21st – June 21st

Planet: Mercury

Element: Air

Mode: Mutable (flexible)

Human Anatomy Association: Shoulders, Upper Arms, and Lungs

Characteristics: Inventive... Adaptable... Cerebral... Good communication skills ... Preoccupied ... Lively... Surface-oriented

Cultivate: Concentration... Ability to relax

Cancer: June 22nd – July 23rd
Planet: Moon
Element: Water
Mode: Cardinal (self-starter)
Human Anatomy Association: Stomach, Breast, Elbows
Characteristics: Emotional... Maternal... Imaginative... Intuitive... Protective
Cultivate: Logic... Emotional stability

Leo: July 24th – August 23rd
Planet: Sun
Element: Fire
Mode: Fixed (immovable)
Human Anatomy Association: Heart, Spine, Upper Back
Characteristics: Leadership ability... Dramatic... Glamour... Confidence... Opinionated
Cultivate: Attention to detail... Humility

Virgo: August 24th – September 23rd
Planet: Mercury
Element: Earth

Mode: Mutable (flexible)

Human Anatomy Association: Intestines, Hands

Characteristics: Organized... Analytical... Self-dedication... Sensible... Finicky

Cultivate: Optimism... Tolerance

Libra: September 24th – October 23rd

Planet: Venus

Element: Air

Mode: Cardinal (self-starter)

Human Anatomy Association: Lower Back and Kidneys

Characteristics: Balanced... Artistic... Easily influenced... Need for companionship... Poised... Diplomatic

Cultivate: Decisiveness... Consistency

Scorpio: October 24th – November 22nd

Planet: Pluto

Element: Water

Mode: Fixed (immovable)

Human Anatomy Association: Reproductive System, Pelvis

Characteristics: Passionate... Pursuit of extremes... Investigative...Jealous... Secretive

Cultivate: Forgiveness... Prioritization of aspirations

Sagittarius: November 23rd – December 22nd

Planet: Jupiter

Element: Fire
Mode: Mutable (flexible)
Human Anatomy Association: Hips, Thighs, Sacral Region
Characteristics: Enthusiastic... Knowledgeable... Candid... Seeks progress... Divergent Luck
Cultivate: Fixed purpose... Restraint

Capricorn: December 23rd – January 20th
Planet: Saturn
Element: Earth
Mode: Cardinal (self-starter)
Human Anatomy Association: Knees, Skeletal Structure
Characteristics: Goal oriented... Efficient... Serious... Professional... Nondescript
Cultivate: Sociability... Effective self-expression

Aquarius: January 21st – February 19th
Planet: Uranus
Element: Air
Mode: Fixed (immovable)
Human Anatomy Association: Calves, Ankles, Circulatory System
Characteristics: Knowledgeable... Personable... Altruistic... Unique...
Love of the unusual... Unemotional
Cultivate: Practical ability... Affection

Pisces: February 20th – March 20th

Planet: Neptune

Element: Water

Mode: Mutable (flexible)

Human Anatomy Association: Feet, Liver, Lymphatic System

Characteristics: Sensitive… Natural healer… Mystical… Imaginative… Whimsical… Easily led

Cultivate: Determination… Concentration

Understanding the characteristics associated with your sun sign can help reveal both positive and negative tendencies of personality. While not all of these tendencies will apply to everyone, trends toward certain behavior and demeanor can be identified, better understood and changed to suit goals in life. Though the moon sign, ascendant, and other planets factor prominently into the complexities of a person's astrological chart, simply knowing someone's sun sign may also help you understand behavior particular to others and adjust your interactions accordingly. For example, if one person – a Virgo – is very analytical and practical, and another – a Sagittarius – is a wayward gambler, then their fate as a couple could face a negative future unless both of them seek to highlight each other's compatible qualities. This route can be accelerated by careful examination of each astrological chart, which will uncover possible conflicts in disposition and help to accept and/or resolve those differences.

The ascendant can help illustrate how someone is perceived by others. It is determined by the specific time of an individual's birth. To determine your ascendant, use the sun sign list to count in order every two hours from 6:00am, starting with your sun sign to the exact time of day you were born (keeping in mind to subtract an hour for daylight saving time, which begins the second Sunday in March and ends the first Sunday in November). For example, if you are a Pisces born at about 3:00pm, begin counting at 6:00am with Pisces, then 8:00am with Aries, 10:00am with Taurus, 12:00pm with Gemini, and end at 2:00pm at Cancer. Because your time of birth is 3:00pm in this example, your ascendant therefore falls between the 2:00pm and 4:00pm, making you a Cancer ascendant. In another example, if you are a Cancer born at 11:15am, begin counting at 6:00am with Cancer, then 8:00am with Leo and 10:00am with Virgo. Since this falls in the summer during daylight savings time between the 10:00am and 12:00pm time period, subtract one hour from the birth time of 11:15am to arrive 10:15am, placing you on the cusp of Leo/Virgo – anything that falls within a few minutes of two different signs can lead to either one being dominant in an individual's character. This is not exact but can give an idea of an individual's ascendant characteristics.

When you have determined both your sun sign and ascendant, refer to the sun sign list found earlier in this chapter and use it again to find out traits common the your ascendant sign. The combination of sun sign and ascendant will shed further light on your personal constitution, adding another dimension to the direction your overall chart takes.

A central piece of an astrological chart are the 12 "houses" that the chart is divided into. Imagine a clock with a compartment between each number. Your ascendant is placed at 9:00 o'clock and then the houses are arranged counter-clockwise in order with each sign following your ascendant. For example, if your ascendant is Scorpio, place Scorpio at 9:00 o'clock, Sagittarius at 8:00, Capricorn at 7:00, Aquarius at 6:00, etc., following the signs in order of the chart above until each of the 12 houses are filled. The planets are placed counter-clockwise into each compartment based on your birth date, time, and place. The reason it is important that an astrologer determines the proper placement of the planets in the houses is because this placement reflects light on the structure of your individual make-up.

1st House: Your ascendant
2nd House: Personal belongings
3rd House: Short travels
4th House: Home
5th House: Pleasures

6th House: Health

7th House: Partnerships

8th House: Passions

9th House: Foreign travels

10th House: Career

11th House: Friends

12th House: Subconscious

For an analysis of your personal astrological chart or a compatibility reading, contact Danielle at stellastarastro@gmail.com.

As is evident, there are many layers to unearth in an astrological reading. Understanding the basic foundations will help you learn more about yourself and discover common ground with others. It is a tool to be paired with other centuries-old systems that will assist us when needed to move confidently in the direction towards a positive path.

Massage

Well Deserved Relaxation

Now, it's time to really relax. Certainly, you don't need a lengthy discourse on the joys of receiving a massage. Here are a few words from our resident massage therapist, Karen Imielinski, followed by a quick series of massage movements that you and a partner can perform at home...

✐**Illustrative Journal: by Karen Imielinski, Massage Therapist**
I love to offer massage therapy at Tranquil Seas Retreats! We all know the physical benefits. Massage helps lower blood pressure, increases metabolism, reduces stress and promotes a feeling of well-being, to name a few benefits. But certainly more than that, it is a truly individual spiritual experience. It brings us closer to our inner-self. It makes us more "body aware." Those who receive a massage often remark about how they didn't realize how stressed they were or how much they really needed their time on the massage table. Many also tell me how they seem to have been transported to a far-away place of peace and tranquility. That is what I love most about massage therapy!

I feel truly blessed to be a conduit for people to receive this experience. This is my intention as I begin each and every massage session. It becomes a stress reducer for me also. As I close the door and enter the massage room, any and all worries or concerns that may be harboring in my mind are left outside the door. They are put on "hold" and allow me to totally focus on my client. It is true "tranquility" for all concerned.

Couples / Partner Massage

A few techniques that can be performed at home…

The following will give you a very basic set of massage techniques that you can use for partner massage. It isn't comprehensive and will not give you enough information to diagnose or to treat any ailments of the musculoskeletal system. It also does not permit you to massage anyone other than your consenting partner.

We realize that all massage is relaxing & enjoyable. It is also very healthful. However, it is important that you know that massage is not always appropriate. In some cases, massage should not be given. Some, but not necessarily all, of the contraindicated conditions are: blood clots, open sores or wounds, recent injuries, systemic infections, cancer, varicose veins, hemophilia.

If you are not sure whether you should be massaging your partner, then don't. Stop and consult a physician.

Where Should I Perform Massage?

Obviously, a massage table is ideal. If you do not have access to a massage table, you can use a single/twin sized bed or use the floor. When using the floor, you begin to tire sooner and experience back fatigue sooner, but it will work.

What Type Of Oil Should I Use?

The most common oils are sweet almond oil, grape seed oil, and apricot oil. All of these can be purchased at health food stores or at bath or body lotion stores.

Step 1: Applying Oil

1. Position yourself at the head of your partner.

2. With the palm of one hand facing upwards, squirt some oil into it and rub your hands together to warm the oil. Do not put too much oil on or it will drip onto the floor.

3. Using short, overlapping strokes, apply oil to the back. Start at the base of the neck and stroke down both sides of the back to the

base of the spine. Keep your hands on the muscular part of the back, avoiding pressure on the spine. Repeat this several times moving slightly outwards each time until you have oiled the entire back.

4. Place more oil in your hand and repeat the short, overlapping strokes down the arms.

5. While applying oil, keep your hands relaxed and use light pressure.

Step 2: Basic Massage Stroke

1. Start at the base of the neck with both hands and use long, gentle strokes down the middle of the back to the base.

2. Move across the "glutes" to the outer hips.

3. Proceed back up the outside edges of the back, across the shoulders and down the arms.

4. Without losing touch with your partner, come back up the arms and across the shoulders again.

5. Finish this long stroke by bringing the hands up the neck to their hairline.

6. Repeat this stroke 3-5 times. Go slowly, there is no need to hurry. You can progressively increase the pressure you use with each stroke.

Step 3: Neck Massage

1. Do not be afraid of massaging the neck. There are numerous muscles in the neck and they carry a large amount of stress.

2. Begin at the base of the skull (along the hairline). Place one on either side of the neck, with your thumbs touching.

3. Stroke down the sides of the neck and fan out along the top of the shoulders.

4. Reverse the stroke back up to the base of the skull again.

5. Use more pressure on the downward (or first half) of this stroke. Use lighter pressure on the return.

6. REPEAT this stroke 3-5 times. You can continue using these two strokes for the entire massage. This is extremely basic but very relaxing and your partner will enjoy its benefits.

Anyone who has ever attended a Tranquil Seas Retreat knows that when optional workshops and wellness services are offered, people rush to the sign-up sheet for a chance to get on Karen's massage table. Contact her at karenski123@verizon.net for a first-hand experience.

Answers To Common Questions

Q: Are Tranquil Seas Retreats non-denominational?

A: Yes. Though spirituality is a frequent topic and discussed in a very broad sense, no specific religious beliefs are taught during classes, aside from lectures on historical religions (such as Zoroastrianism or Taoism), which are presented for educational purposes only. We strive to make our events as all-inclusive as possible and encourage a wide variety of beliefs and philosophies amongst our participants.

Q: What if I don't want to do Yoga/Qigong/Guitar/Whatever?

A: There are always plenty or workshops and classes scheduled at Tranquil Seas Retreats. If you are not interested in one of them, the weekend is yours to do what you want with it, whether you want to take a nature walk, craft with beads, or simply enjoy the company of others in the den. It is also our policy that if a class is on a topic that is very specific (e.g. the guitar workshop) we offer a different class in the same time slot, so that there are always plenty of choices available and plenty to do.

Q: Are Tranquil Seas Retreats for ladies only?

A: Primarily, yes, Tranquil Seas Retreats are ladies only, though we occasionally organize mixed-gender events. Whether the retreat is only for ladies, or also for men, will be indicated on our website and registration materials.

Q: We're anxious to get there. How early can we arrive?

A: Arrival times will be addressed in the preparatory email we send out prior to each retreat, but as a general rule, someone from the Tranquil Seas Retreat staff will be there to welcome you by Noon of the scheduled start day.

Q: Will I have to carry my own luggage?

A: No, the guitar teacher will do that for you. Pack as many personal belongings as you like, he can handle it.

Q: What if I want to carry my own luggage? I don't need any help.

A: The guitar guy is still going to carry your luggage. He's stubborn.

Q: Are the rooms single or double occupancy?

A: Whether the rooms are single or double occupancy depend on the location of the retreat. If the location is set up for double occupancy style lodging, if you contact us prior to registering and request a single occupancy room, we will make every effort to accommodate any special needs.

Q: Is the food mostly vegetarian?

A: No. There is usually some type of meat, poultry, or fish served at least once per day. In addition, vegetable-based dishes are always served at each meal. Anyone with very specific nutritional requirements (such as gluten-free diets) is welcome to bring supplementary food and give it to the kitchen staff for refrigerated storage.

Q: If I speak my mind while holding the "Talking Stick," will it lead to contentious debates with other members of the group?

A: The purpose of the Talking Stick is for you to speak and others to listen. Not many people resort to inflammatory speech during that particular activity, as everyone realizes the purpose of the weekend is for relaxation. You will find that while on a mountaintop or at the seashore, hundreds of miles away from their common stressors, very few people can maintain the level of agitation necessary to make remarks like

"The President is an idiot." Some people think our current President is an idiot, others believe our prior President was an idiot. A third group feel that both of them are idiots. The point is, by the time you get the Talking Stick in your hand, hours of Yoga, and guided meditation will probably have caused you to temporarily forget exactly who the President is.

Q: Can I host a retreat in my area?

A: If you have a group of people 25 or more in number, and you would like to host a retreat near your home, we can arrange to bring our staff to your location and organize a retreat at a mutually agreed upon facility. Standard classes include yoga, qigong, meditation, reiki, and communication workshop. Customized activities can also be arranged. For more detailed information on hosting retreats, contact us through our website, www.masteringtranquility.com

✍ Illustrative Journal: by N. C.

What is so special about a women's retreat? It is somewhat of a mystery. We often come from vastly different worlds. We often come for many different reasons: fun, escape, healing, learning, renewal, friendship. It is usually difficult for us to come to such an event. Our jobs, families and responsibilities always seem to take priority. Women rarely set their own needs before others.

The fact that we have made a commitment to give ourselves a break and have taken the long drive to arrive at a beautiful destination is a feat in and of itself. By the first evening, the room is alive with the excited hum of women's voices and laughter. Dress shoes and designer clothes have been traded in for sneakers and sweat pants and we have all decided to let our hair down. For me, it was as though I was back at a slumber party with my best friends in high school. Our conversations were just as passionate and our laughter just as loud. Stories of love, loss and heartache are a bit more real to us now. Most of us have lived through it. We are more appreciative of this time with one another as we realize that it may have been years since we have given ourselves permission for such an indulgence.

It cannot just be taken for granted that when a group of women get together, there is a magical healing process that occurs. This is a result of a carefully created retreat atmosphere. Nora sets her intention to create a space of healing, openness and acceptance and what follows is the magic that occurs on a Tranquil Seas Retreat. From the moment one enters, there is a feeling of being accepted and welcomed to a place of trust, acceptance and friendship. Nora is right there mingling with the group and having fun right along with us.

No one is set above anyone else. Each of our experiences and insights are relevant and valuable. The women who are teaching and presenting for the weekend are carefully chosen to reflect Nora's vision for the retreat. No one is obligated to attend every event. The retreat is what we make of it. Some choose to be more solitary and introspective. Some are grieving the loss of a loved one and take comfort in the strength that comes from being surrounded by women. There is no judgment, we simply come as we are. I have been to many wonderful presentations, classes and destinations at Tranquil Seas Retreats. When asked what my favorite event would be, I would have to say, hands down, spending a weekend with a group of amazing women. What I always bring home from these retreats is strength from our resilience and healing from our laughter.

Q: What can I hope to gain by attending a Tranquil Seas Retreat?

A: Attending a Tranquil Seas Retreat can show you the way to stress-reduction, self-advancement, healing, revitalization, introduce you to new interests, or simply help you to meet like-minded people who are on similar life-paths. Our journeys include a medley of activities that you can view as a buffet, or explore all of them. The one common thread is bringing you into balance. As you've learned from earlier chapters of this book, this can be accomplished in many different ways. We show you how to change things that you didn't believe you could change. Control elements that were once viewed as uncontrollable. Demonstrate that it is never too late to turn life in the direction of positivity, no matter what has transpired in the past. We do so by proverbially "teaching you how to fish," then by going fishing alongside you, with a group of wonderful people that can help demonstrate how to move forward in life, because they have done so themselves, often through great adversity. And we have fun in the process.

✐Illustrative Journal: by A. M. Revello

Just wanted to let you know how terrific the presentations and the whole weekend were again. Dave's guitar workshops are terrific, he makes it interesting and informative for all levels and has useful tips. I really enjoyed Nora's talk on Zoroastrianism – it was an interesting topic but her enthusiasm and knowledge of the subject are what make the talks so enjoyable. The self-protection class was very informative and helpful. Toni's life transitions talk was wonderful as well, and it is a subject that applies to everyone. What I learned from the self-protection and the life transitions classes alone were both potentially life changing. That's a lot to be able to learn from one weekend. Add to that a group of fabulous and fun women and you can't beat it!

Taking the Next Step

Your life is within your control.

It's never too late to transform yourself into a more complete person. In fact, the process just may be easier than you think. Though you are encouraged to engage in a lifetime of good habits, the positive changes you see may happen quicker than you ever thought possible. Embrace new directions and new ideas. Become a well-rounded human being by learning new skills and sharing them with others.

✐Illustrative Journal: by Sheryl M.
One of the best parts of the Tranquil Seas Retreats is the energy that each different group has. It's unique each time. There's a connection that is deep each time, but it's not quite like any other time. The group begins bonding with the opening session. Each experience we share creates bonds between the women, but also deepens the group energy. I think that's why, by the last session – new friendships have been made, lessons understood, older friendships strengthened.

It's a wonderful balance of learning, laughing and growing. I love the variety of topics presented. I love to learn about new things. I find it fascinating to learn from a person who LOVES the subject. That makes it so much more interesting.

There never seems to be enough time to explore all the exciting hobbies and interests that are out there. And I love to try new things. Many of the topics were things that I was hoping to learn about. It's always fun to find that a new friend has a quirky hobby or is an expert in an unusual area.

In This Technological Age, People Still Have Actual Faces

In an ironic twist, the always unreliable fiber-optic network, which shall go unnamed (but rhymes with "Horizon") has gone out for the day, during the writing of this book's concluding chapter. While having no internet, television, or telephone may be viewed as a problem by some, the lack of distractions more than makes up for the inconvenience of temporarily not being able to use email to accept illustrative journal submissions from this book's contributors. Instead, today the internet has been entirely replaced by a paper dictionary, and actual face-to-face communication.

Sometimes less technology means less stress – especially when it affords us the time to engage in the near forgotten art of conversation. We are social beings, and that means interaction that goes beyond the conveniences of email and text messaging. That is one of the major reasons we travel to mountaintops and seashores, far away from the distractions of modern life, to meaningfully connect with others and share our positive energy.

✎Illustrative Journal: by Karen Imielinski

One of my favorite things about retreats is the camaraderie. Having been a wife and mother for the past forty years, I have managed to put everyone else's needs and wants first. Hence, my needs and wants were put on "hold." This is of my own doing. But when the chance to go away with friends for a weekend became available, I took advantage.

I did not realize how much I missed the engaging relationship of women friends. It has become a joy to spend this time with such marvelous people. We laugh and cry together. We "eat, pray and love" together! We are an extremely eclectic group of women from many different walks in life, yet we have one thing in common…we love life! We love energy work, we love to learn new things and expand our horizons.

Getting up early in the morning and practicing yoga either on a mountain top or on the beach is exhilarating. A great start to any morning! Raising your vibrations sets the stage for your day. All of the lectures and/or keynote speakers are excellent. One of my favorites would be palmistry. Learning the meaning of the lines of your palms is quite interesting. Your life is an open book shown in your palm. We have been blessed to have speakers on grief counseling, homeopathy, and Zoroastrianism to name just a few. Quite a wide spectrum of interesting experiences. If that weren't enough, we also practice different energy and bodywork modalities. We have received Reiki, and massage therapy. All are done by certified therapists.

Tranquil Seas Retreat...what a perfect name! It is so much more than a weekend away. It affords spiritual and mental enrichment. It allows time for reflection with quiet time and beautiful walks through nature or through a meditative labyrinth. It gives us time to learn new things with great keynote speakers. We also have some really fun workshops! I have had an opportunity to learn to play guitar in the guitar workshop. That has proved to be a jump start to a new hobby! And let us not forget the fun of "dancing to the tunes" in the evening after all of our "learning" has been concluded.

Please Take The Following Advice Very Seriously.

The very next thing you read is the most important sentence in this book.

BE GOOD TO YOURSELF.

Those four words are the best advice anyone can ever give you. Though it may mean different things to different people, the preceding chapters have given you a broad basis to move forward with whichever combination of techniques and practices you wish to pursue.

Being good to yourself is a requirement, not an option.

It is your right, not to be viewed as privilege.

The consequences of not doing so can be devastating. Is there any logical reason anyone can come up with that argues against making good nutritional intake and adequate sleep high, if not the highest two priorities in a human being's life? Even the staunchest opponent of Abraham Maslow and his famous "Hierarchy of Needs" would find it impossible to argue otherwise, yet many people still choose to push absolutely essential components of happiness to the back of the line. If someone were to tell you that they sleep no more than four hours per night, eat fast-food every day, and spend hours each evening sitting in a dimly lit room drinking beverages that make the simple act of driving home dangerous to everyone around them…well, what would you assume would be the effect on their general health? Their mental health? Their physical appearance? Are the answers anything but obvious? Yet every one of us is acquainted with individuals who treat themselves with utter disregard. Don't be one of them. Your life is a gift. Treat it with respect.

Help others by, likewise, helping yourself.

In the event that you have small children, are a caretaker to an elderly relative, or are in a relationship where circumstances require you to give of yourself to an extraordinary degree, you may find yourself rationalizing that you can't put the requisite amount of effort in to taking care of yourself due to various incidents that occur.

Rest assured that if your main focus is to serve the ones who find themselves in your immediate care, that you will be of much more capable assistance to them if you are functioning at your highest level. They will likely be the first ones to remind you to eat three balanced meals a day and give yourself the opportunity to sleep at least seven hours a night.

On the flip-side of that coin, you will also encounter those who don't care about your well-being nearly as much as whatever your particular value is to them. It goes without saying that it can become very necessary to retain your vision of where you want your life to go and not permit anyone else to alter it against your will.

Fight back when necessary.

While you may assign varying levels of personal importance to outside stressors such as an overbearing boss screaming about arbitrary (and often meaningless) project deadlines, or creditors calling a dozen times a day to inform you that you are two days late in paying a credit card bill at the exorbitant 30% interest rate they have decided to charge you, rest assured that while these events may be unpleasant, they have no more importance in your life than you allow them to.

Fight back when the situation calls for it. How you do so is a matter of personal style. Some choose to simply ignore those who harass them, in the hope of a peaceful diffusion. Others will take a more forceful approach. Be certain not to mistake tranquility for passivity. Watch how a prizefighter in a boxing match remains calm in the face of physical attack. Though the example may be extreme, it is fantastic and powerful illustration of finding stillness in the whirlwind.

Remain calm through adversity.

Easier said than done? Certainly.

Absolutely necessary? Yes.

When things go wrong, those who not only survive, but flourish under difficulty are the ones who can calmly execute their plan of action. When hard times hit, take out a pen and paper and make a list of what you need to do. Then make a list of what you shouldn't do. Stick to the plan. Trust in yourself that you have chosen the right path, and don't let anyone talk you out of it.

Have confidence in yourself.

You are strong. You are capable of leadership. You are capable of accomplishing everything you want out of life. Do not doubt yourself. Doubt accomplishes nothing. Furthermore, it is counterproductive.

Instead, motivate yourself. Do it any way possible. Do it for your spouse, your children, your grandchildren, your pets, and, most importantly, yourself.

Be realistic, but at the same time, be self-assured. Envision yourself as you would like to be, and do not give up that vision. Mental visualization is a powerful tool, and will assist you in prevailing when things become problematic.

Exercise your will.

Stand up to the negativities that each day will assault you with. Don't let outside circumstances dictate how you feel on the inside. You have a choice in the matter. Once you have overcome a bad situation once, it will be easier to do the next time. And even easier each subsequent time after that. Struggle will always precede great accomplishment. Through it all, continue to move forward.

Realize your immense importance in this world.

It is tremendously inaccurate to ever think that your place on this Earth is not one of great importance. Whether you realize it or not, you have touched people's lives with your presence. Taking good care of your mind, body, and spirit will allow you to live your life filled with abundance and continue to touch others with love and radiate humble appreciation for all the wonderful gifts in your life.

Let your good deeds be their own reward, and you will find yourself fostering wonderful relationships in the process.

Move forward.

Use this book to begin a life-long journey to emotional balance, physical wellness, spiritual fulfillment, and a life filled with abundance. The skills you acquire will serve you well as you overcome stressors and master tranquility.

We'll see you on the mountain.

Acknowledgements

It is said that friends are our chosen families. This could not be more true in my case. The concept of being a midlife orphan is not a prominent topic in any social circle, but once my parents had both passed I wanted to create a family unit. Of course, this included my life-long buddies, Dr. William Forstchen, Joan Minneci and Mike D'Ecclesis to whom I will be forever grateful for their unwavering friendship.

I wish to thank my husband and dearest friend David for always having my back and supporting my endeavors full throttle. I met him at 16, married at 19 and had my family unit. Things only got better when our son Dave joined us, who now as an adult has become my closest advisor and co-director of Tranquil Seas Retreats. I am blessed. When I returned to the East from living in California, I met the most amazing group of people, who continue to be a huge part of my life as well as members of the Tranquil Seas Retreat journeys.

Joan Barrett, Susan Gdovin, Karen Imielinski, Dr. Gloria Lopez, Sheryl Mitchell, Greg Mitrosky, Janice Prodell, Barbara Snow, Michele Wosak.

Finally, to the Tranquil Seas presenters who contributed to this book, without whom the retreats would not be the success that they are: Barb, Danielle, Dave, Karen, Jeannie, Michele, Toni.

About the Author

As the owner and administrator of "Tranquil Seas" Retreats, Nora D'Ecclesis has a long history of presenting events focused on wellness and stress reduction techniques. A typical Tranquil Seas Retreat is a weekend-long group getaway to the beach or mountains, during which experts in each particular discipline treat attendees to a selection of lectures and activities that give them the knowledge to advance their lives physically, emotionally and spiritually.

Nora has compiled a variety of effective techniques and practices and illuminated them in her books, "Mastering Tranquility," "Tranquil Seas," and "Reiki Roundtable."

Nora is a graduate of Kean University, also holding a graduate degree in education, post-graduate certification as a learning specialist, and the rank of Shihan as a Usui Reiki Master. She enjoys canoeing, fishing and archery. Nora lives with her family in a suburb of Philadelphia, Pennsylvania.

For more information, visit www.noradecclesis.com or contact her by email at noradecclesis@gmail.com

NOTES

www.ingramcontent.com/pod-product-compliance
Lightning Source LLC
LaVergne TN
LVHW051825080426
835512LV00018B/2734